COMPUTATIONAL

COMPUTATIONAL
THINKING

PETER J. DENNING AND
MATTI TEDRE

The MIT Press | Cambridge, Massachusetts | London, England

© 2019 The Massachusetts Institute of Technology

All rights reserved. No part of this book may be reproduced in any form
by any electronic or mechanical means (including photocopying, recording,
or information storage and retrieval) without permission in writing from
the publisher.

This book was set in Chaparral Pro by Toppan Best-set Premedia Limited.
Printed and bound in the United States of America.

Library of Congress Cataloging-in-Publication Data

Names: Denning, Peter J., 1942- author. | Tedre, Matti, author.
Title: Computational thinking / Peter J. Denning and Matti Tedre.
Description: Cambridge, MA : The MIT Press, 2019. | Series: The MIT press
    essential knowledge series | Includes bibliographical references and index.
Identifiers: LCCN 2018044011 | ISBN 9780262536561 (pbk. : alk. paper)
Subjects: LCSH: Computer algorithms—Popular works. | Computer logic—
    Popular works. | Electronic data processing—Social aspects—Popular
    works.
Classification: LCC QA76.9.L63 D46 2019 | DDC 005.1—dc23 LC record
    available at https://lccn.loc.gov/2018044011

10   9   8   7   6   5   4   3   2   1

CONTENTS

SERIES FOREWORD

The MIT Press Essential Knowledge series offers accessible, concise, beautifully produced pocket-size books on topics of current interest. Written by leading thinkers, the books in this series deliver expert overviews of subjects that range from the cultural and the historical to the scientific and the technical.

In today's era of instant information gratification, we have ready access to opinions, rationalizations, and superficial descriptions. Much harder to come by is the foundational knowledge that informs a principled understanding of the world. Essential Knowledge books fill that need. Synthesizing specialized subject matter for nonspecialists and engaging critical topics through fundamentals, each of these compact volumes offers readers a point of access to complex ideas.

Bruce Tidor
Professor of Biological Engineering and Computer Science
Massachusetts Institute of Technology

A computer revolution is in full swing. The invasion of computing into every part of our lives has brought enormous benefits including email, internet, World Wide Web, Amazon's e-commerce, Kahn Academy, Uber's taxi hailing, Google's maps, trip navigators, smartphones, real-time translators, and apps by the millions. At the same time it has also brought enormous concerns including possible loss of jobs to automation, mass surveillance, collapse of critical infrastructure, cyber war, mass sales of personal data, invasions of advertising, loss of privacy, polarization of politics, loss of civility and respectful listening, and exacerbated income inequality.

A lot of people are having trouble coming to grips with all this. Can they reap the benefits without the downside costs? Can they lead a meaningful life if computerization suddenly threatens to obsolete a lifetime of learning? What should their children learn about computing to enable them to move and prosper in the new world?

Computational thinking is a new term that has recently entered public discourse as people struggle with these questions. It holds the hope that we can think clearly about the powers and dangers of mass computing, and that we can learn to design computers, software, and networks to maximize the benefits and minimize the risks. Parents are already amazed at how facile their children seem to be in the digital world. Is computational thinking the recipe for giving our children a proper education in this world?

We designed this book to be an edifying conversation to help you understand what computational thinking is so that you will be in a better position to answer these questions for yourself.

The first thing to understand is that a substantial part of daily discourse is shaped by the wide adoption of computers. This is nothing new; our ancestors' ways of thinking about the world were shaped by the technologies of previous revolutions. In the industrial age, for example, people regularly used expressions like

"He blew a gasket,"

"I'm humming on all pistons,"

"It's a high pressure environment," and

"I had to blow off steam."

Today we hear expressions like

"My DNA programs me to do it this way,"

"Our laws are algorithms for running our society,"

"My brain is hardware and my mind software," and

"My brain crashed, I need to reboot."

Just as in the industrial age, the new idioms of the computer age reveal more about our popular culture than they do about the technology.

Like the Greek god Janus, computational thinking has two faces, one that looks behind and explains all that has happened, and one that looks ahead to what can be designed. We invoke both faces when we want to get computers to do jobs for us. On the back-facing side, we need to understand the mechanics of how computers work, how they are controlled by algorithms, how we can express algorithms in a programming language, and how we can combine many software modules into working systems. On the forward-facing side, we need sensibilities to understand the context in which users of our software are working. We want our software to be valuable to them and not to cause harm to them or their environment. Thus, computational thinking guides us to understand the technology available to us and to design software to do a job or solve a problem.

Computational thinking is not only something programmers must know, but it is also a thinking tool for understanding our technology-infused social world. It increases our awareness of how our everyday digital tools work, grounds our cyber ethics, and improves our resilience against various threats such as algorithm-driven attempts to guide our behavior, personally tailored fake news, viral powers of social media, and massive, data-intensive analysis of our movements. What is more, computational thinking has irrevocably changed the tools, methods, and epistemology of science. Learning CT has many benefits beyond programming.

If you try to understand what computational thinking is from media accounts, you will hear a story of problem solving with algorithms, along with the ability to think at the many levels of abstraction needed to solve problems. The story is flavored with images of joyous children having fun programming and playing games in which they simulate algorithms. Indeed, our teachers have learned much about computational thinking from teaching computing to children, and they have developed superb ways of teaching fundamental computing insights to newcomers. In this book, we call this "CT for beginners."

But the K–12 education insights and debates barely scratch the surface of computational thinking. At the more advanced levels, computational thinking concerns the design of hardware, networks, storage systems, operating systems, and the cloud. Its historical predecessors have organized human teams to do large computations, organized production lines in manufacturing, guided lawmakers, and specified the rules of bureaucracies. It has developed styles attuned to major areas where computing plays a critical role, such as artificial intelligence, large data analytics, software engineering, and computational science. We will show you all this by examining the kinds of computational thinking needed to deal with these different dimensions of computing. A much more advanced kind of computational thinking is needed to deal with these areas. We call it "CT for professionals."

Computational thinking is sometimes portrayed as a universal approach to problem solving. Take a few programming courses, the story in the popular media goes, and you will be able to solve problems in any field. Would that this were true! Your ability to solve a problem for someone depends on your understanding of their context in which the problem exists. For instance, you cannot build simulations of aircraft in flight without understanding fluid dynamics. You cannot program searches through genome databases without understanding the biology of the genome and the methods of collecting the data. Computational thinking is powerful, but not universal.

Computational thinking illuminates a fundamental difference in the ways that humans and machines process information. Machines can process information at billions or trillions of calculations per second, whereas humans do well at one calculation per second. Machines process with no understanding of the data they are processing, whereas humans do and can correct errors on the fly. Machines can transform a mistake in an algorithm into a costly disaster before any human has a chance to react. Thinkers in the philosophy of mind, neuropsychology, cognitive science, and artificial intelligence have studied these differences and shown us how fundamentally dissimilar they are. Although some human tasks like searching and sorting can be eased by applying algorithms to them, most computational thinking in the big picture is concerned with machine computation.

Think for a moment about the speed issue. A typical computer can, in 1 second, perform a billion calculations and draw a complex image on the screen. A human would need 100 years to carry out the same steps at human speed. Humans obviously draw pictures much faster than that, but machine designers have yet to imitate that human capacity. If humans had no help from computers, we would have no real time graphics. Nearly everything we see software doing is made possible by the incredible speeds of computers. These machines, not humans executing algorithms on their own, are the reason for the computer revolution. Computing machines do the humanly impossible.

While this may send a thrill up your neck, it ought also to send a shiver down your spine. Modern aircraft are controlled by networks of computers performing billions of calculations per second. A mistake in an algorithm can cause the control system to send the aircraft into a death spiral long before the human pilot can react. Early Apollo missions and more recent Mars missions were aborted and lost due to errors in their software. Mistakes in algorithms can be deadly and costly. How can we know that the algorithms running critical systems can be trusted to work properly, bringing benefits and low risk of harm? We need clear thinking to help us find our way through this maze of complexity. This requires an advanced form of CT that is not learned from children's simulation games. "CT for professionals" is deadly serious.

Our account of CT in this book encompasses all the flavors of CT from beginners to professionals, and in major subfields such as software engineering and computational science. We aim to describe CT in all its richness, breadth, and depth. We want to celebrate the work of expert professionals who take on the hard challenges of getting complex systems to perform reliably and safely, and the kinds of thinking they bring that enables them to have achieved such a good track record. We also want to celebrate the work of expert educators who are working to ease the first steps into computational thinking in K–12 schools and lay the foundation to provide everyone the means for coping in the digital world. Those two, basic CT for beginners and advanced CT for professionals, work together to produce a rich tapestry of computational thought.

Peter J. Denning
Salinas, California, August 2018

Matti Tedre
Joensuu, Finland, August 2018

ACKNOWLEDGMENTS

Peter: Many thanks to Dorothy Denning, my wife, who listened to my many speeches about computing for nearly 50 years and kept me channeled in productive directions. Much appreciation to my friend Fernando Flores, for teaching me how to read history for the concerns that emerge from it and thus discern different stages of computational thinking over the centuries. To the founders of computing and computing education whom I met through ACM, including Eckert, Mauchly, Perlis, Newell, Simon, Forsythe, Conte, Wilkes, Hamming, Knuth, and Dijkstra. To my teachers at MIT who turned this electrical engineer into one of the first holders of a computer science degree, especially Fano, Corbato, Dennis, Saltzer, Scherr, and Zadeh. To my many colleagues in computer science and engineering over the years, too numerous to mention by name here, who engaged me in edifying conversations about computing.

Matti: I am grateful to all those who have helped me develop my own computational thinking: my old teachers, mentors, and past and present colleagues from all walks of research. I feel privileged to have gained a wealth of computing insights from working in universities in six countries on three continents. I am also thankful to my friends and colleagues from the field of history and philosophy of computer science—too many to be listed here. I wish to especially thank Maarten Bullynck, Edgar Daylight, Liesbeth De Mol, Lauri Malmi, John Pajunen, Giuseppe Primiero, and Simon (as well as ANR PROGRAMme ANR-17-CE38-0003-01 partners) for inspiring conversations, feedback, and collaboration on material directly related to this book. My work was partially supported by the Association of Finnish Non-fiction Writers.

Acknowledgment of prior publishers: Parts of chapter 5 are adapted from the following sources: Great *Principles of Computing* by Peter Denning and Craig Martell (MIT Press, 2015); "The Forgotten Engineer" by Peter Denning (*Communications of the ACM 60*, 12 [December 2017]: 20–23), and "Computing as Engineering" by Matti Tedre (*Journal of Universal Computer Science 15*, 8: 1642–1658). Parts of chapter 6 are adapted from: "Software Quality" by Peter Denning (*Communications of the ACM 59*, 9 [September 2016]: 23–25; "Design Thinking" by Peter Denning (*Communications of the ACM 56*, 12 [December 2013]: 29–31; and Great *Principles of Computing*. Parts of chapter 7 have been adapted from "Computational Thinking in Science" by Peter Denning (*American Scientist 105* [January–February 2017): 13–17.

WHAT IS COMPUTATIONAL THINKING?

An algorithm is a set of rules for getting a specific output from a specific input. Each step must be so precisely defined that it can be translated into computer language and executed by machine.

—Donald Knuth (1977)

What is a computer? Most people will answer it is an electronic black box that does amazing things by collecting, storing, retrieving, and transforming data. Almost all our devices and gadgets are computers: phones, tablets, desktops, web pages, watches, navigators, thermometers, medical devices, clocks, televisions, DVD players, WiFi networks. Our services are software—bookstores, retail stores, banks, transportation, Uber, hotel reservations, Airbnb, filmmaking, entertainment, Dropbox, online courses, Google searches—and almost all run by unseen computers across an unseen worldwide network called "the cloud." Computers have brought enormous benefits—new jobs, access to information, economic development, national defense, improvements in health, and much more. They have brought, as well, worrying concerns—job losses, globalization, privacy, surveillance, and more. It looks like everything that can be digitized is being digitized and computers are everywhere storing and transforming that information. A computer revolution is truly upon us.

How shall we think about all this? What do we need to understand about computers? What must we do to put a computer to work for us? How do computers shape the way we see the world? What new do we see? What is the role of programming? What are computers not good for?

The Power and Value of Computation

Computational thinking (here abbreviated CT) offers some answers to these questions. Much of CT is specifically oriented on figuring out how to get a computer to do a job for us—how to control a complex electronic device to do a job reliably without causing damage or harm. Algorithms are the procedures that specify how the computer should do a job. Although humans can carry out algorithms, they cannot do so nearly as fast as a machine; modern computers can do a trillion steps in the time it takes a human to do one step. The magic is nothing more than a machine executing large numbers of very simple computations very fast. Programs are the bridge: algorithms encoded in special-purpose languages that translate to machine instructions that control a computer.

But CT reaches further than automation. Information and computational processes have become a way of understanding natural and social phenomena. Much of CT today is oriented toward learning how the world works. A growing number of biologists, physicists, chemists, and other scientists are looking at their subject matter through a computational lens; professionals in the arts, humanities, and social sciences are joining in. Computer simulation enables previously impossible virtual experiments. The "information interpretation" of the world offers conceptual and empirical tools that no other approach does.

CT also advises us about jobs that computers cannot do in any reasonable amount of time. Or at all—some jobs are impossible for computers. Many social, political, and economic problems are beyond the pale of computers. By understanding the limits of computing, we can avoid the trap of looking to computing technology to solve such problems.

Obviously, designing a program or a machine to do so much in such a short time is a daunting design task that demands its own way of thinking if we are to have any confidence that the machine does the job without error. Indeed, understanding users, and designing systems specifically for them, turns out to be one of the great challenges of modern computing. Design is one of the central concerns of CT.

Defining Computational Thinking

Computational thinking has become a buzzword with a multitude of definitions. We have distilled the spirit of the multitude into this definition used throughout this book:

Computational thinking is the mental skills and practices for

• *designing* computations that get computers to do jobs for us, and

• *explaining* and interpreting the world as a complex of information processes.

The design aspect reflects the engineering tradition of computing in which people build methods and machines to help other people. The explanation aspect reflects the science tradition of computing in which people seek to understand how computation works and how it shows up in the world. *Design* features immersion in the community being helped, *explanation* features being a dispassionate external observer. In principle, it is possible to design computations without explaining them, or explain computations without designing them. In practice, these two aspects go hand in hand.

Computations are complex series of numerical calculations and symbol manipulations. Examples of numerical calculations are the basic arithmetic operations (add, subtract, multiply, divide) and the basic trigonometric functions (sine, cosine, and tangent). Examples of symbolic manipulations are logical comparison of numbers or symbols, decisions of what instructions to do next, or substitutions of one string of letters and numbers for another. Amazing computations can be carried out when trillions of such simple operations are arranged in the proper order—for example, forecasting tomorrow's weather, deciding where to drill for oil, designing the wings of an aircraft with enough lift to fly, finding which physical places are most likely to be visited by a person, calling for a taxi, or figuring out which two people would make a great couple.

Computers are agents that carry out the operations of a computation. They follow programs of instructions for doing arithmetic and logic operations. Computers can be humans or machines. Humans can follow programs, but are nowhere near as fast or as error-free as machines.

Machines can perform computational feats well beyond human capabilities.

We use the word "job" to refer to any task that someone considers valuable. Today many people look to computers (actually, computations performed by computers) to get jobs done. They seek automation of jobs that could not be done without the aid of a machine. Computers are now getting good enough at some routine jobs so that loss of employment to automation has become an important social concern.

We do not equate "doing a job" with automation. Well-defined, routine jobs can be automated, but ill-defined jobs such as "meeting a concern" cannot. CT can help with jobs that cannot be automated. In the design chapter we will discuss the kind of CT that does this.

There is clearly a special thinking skill required to successfully design programs and machines capable of enormous computations and to understand natural information processes through computation. This skill—computational thinking, or CT—is not a set of concepts for programming. Instead, CT comprises ways of thinking and practicing that are sharpened and honed through practice. CT is a very rich skill set: at the end of this chapter we outline the six dimensions of computational thinking that you will encounter in this book: machines, methods, computing education, software engineering, design, and computational science.

Wishful Thinking

In our enthusiasm for computational thinking, we need to be careful to avoid wishful thinking. Perhaps the first and most common wish is that we can get computers to do any job we can conceive of. This wish cannot be realized because there are many jobs that are impossible for computers. For example, there is no algorithm that will inspect another algorithm and tell us whether it terminates or loops forever. Every programming student longs for such an algorithm to help with debugging. It was logically impossible in 1936 when Alan Turing proved it so, and it is still impossible today.

Even if we stick to logically possible jobs, there are many that cannot be done in a reasonable time—they are intractable. One famous example is the traveling salesman problem, which is to find the shortest tour on a map of a country that visits each city just once. An algorithm to compute this would be of great value in the package delivery industry. The simplest way to find the shortest tour is to enumerate all possible tours and select the shortest. For a small set of 100 cities, this would take 10^{130} years on the world's fastest supercomputer. For comparison the age of the universe is on the order of 10^{10} years. Even the "simplest way" can be impossible! Algorithms analysts have identified thousands of common problems that are intractable in this way.

The picture gets even more confusing because in most cases there are fast algorithms to find an approximate answer. They are called heuristics. Take, for example, the problem of finding the shortest tour connecting all 24,978 cities in Sweden. The enumeration algorithm for the traveling salesman problem would take on the order of $10^{100,000}$ years! But in 2004 a team at the University of Waterloo using heuristics for optimization found a shortest tour and proved it to be correct. Their solution used 85 years of processing time spread over a cluster of machines that took several months to complete the job.

Computational thinkers need to develop enough experience and skill to know when jobs are impossible or intractable, and look for good heuristics to solve them.

A second example of wishful thinking is to believe that learning how to program in a computer science course or a coding-intensive workshop will enable you to solve problems in any field that uses computation. No, you will need to learn something about the other field too. For example, even if you have studied search algorithms in a programming course, you are not likely to be able to be useful to a genomics project until you have learned genome biology and the significance of biological data.

A third example of wishful thinking is to believe that computers are not essential to CT—that we can think about how to solve problems with algorithms and not be concerned with the computers that run the algorithms.

But this is not so. When a computer does not have sufficient memory to hold all your data, you will seek ways to divide your problem into subsets that will fit. When a single processor does not have sufficient processing power, you will seek a computer with multiple parallel processors and algorithms that divide the computation among them. When the computer is too slow, you will look inside to find a bottlenecked component and either upgrade it or find a new algorithm that does not use that component. Even if your computer has sufficient memory, adequate processing power, and no bottlenecks, other aspects can limit your problem-solving progress, notably the speed of the internal clock, which paces the machine to perform computational steps in an orderly and predictable way. But some new machines, notably quantum computers and neural nets, have no clocks: How shall we think about programming them?

A fourth example of wishful thinking is to believe the computer is smart. If you are imprecise in translating human steps into program steps, your computation will contain errors that could cause disasters. Computers are incredibly dumb. They perform mindless, mechanical steps extremely fast but they have no understanding of what the steps mean. The only errors they can correct are the ones you anticipate and provide with corrective algorithms. You are the source of the intelligence; the computer amplifies your intelligence but has none of its own.

We advise you to approach CT with humility. It is a learned skill. Our brains do not naturally think computationally. Keep your perspective on the capabilities of computers and algorithms to do jobs, on the need to learn something about the application domain you want to design for, on the dependency of computation on computers, and the abject lack of intelligence in the machine.

Emergence of CT over Millennia

It might seem that CT is a product of the electronic computer age that began in the 1940s. Well, not really. Before the modern computer age there was a profession of mathematically trained experts who performed complex calculations as teams. They were called "computers." They were by no means the first: the term "computer," meaning "one who computes," dates back to the early 1600s. The first electronic computing machines were called automatic computers to distinguish them from the human variety. Human computers and, even more so, the leaders of human computing teams, obviously engaged in computational thinking. So, many aspects of CT existed before electronic computers. Well before.

Primitive forms of CT as methods of calculation were recorded from around 1800 to 1600 BCE among the Babylonians, who wrote down general procedures for solving mathematical problems. Their rule-following procedures have features that we, from today's perspective, would label as forms of CT. Similarly, the Egyptian engineers who built the pyramids beginning around 2700 BCE obviously knew a lot about geometry and were able to calculate the dimensions and angles of stones for each part of the pyramid and of the leverage of ropes, pulleys, and rollers to move the stones into position. Computing is an ancient human practice.

Over the ages since ancient times, mathematicians sought to spell out procedures for ever more advanced calculations, moving beyond calculating merchant transactions and the geometry of structures, to trigonometry, astronomic predictions, celestial navigation, solving algebraic equations, and eventually computing with the calculus of Newton and Leibniz. By formalizing computing procedures, mathematicians made their expertise available to non-experts who simply had to follow directions of carrying out simple arithmetic operations in the proper order. A special class of those directions is today called an algorithm—a key concept in modern computing. The term "algorithm" comes to us from the Persian mathematician Muhammad ibn Mūsā al-Khwārizmī who, around 800 CE, discussed how to formulate mathematical procedures and gave examples such as finding the greatest common divisor of a set of numbers.

We humans have a penchant for automating routine procedures. So it has been for computational procedures: inventors sought machines that would automate computation for the purposes of greater speed and fewer errors. Building machines to carry out these procedures turned out to be much harder than specifying the procedures. Pascal designed and built an arithmetic machine in the 1600s that was able to add and subtract. It could multiply only in the hands of a human operator who understood repeated addition. It could not do division. Napier invented the logarithm, which became the principle of the slide rule—an aid for calculation that continued well into the second half of the 1900s. It could not add or subtract. In 1819 Babbage designed a machine of gears, shafts, and wheels that could calculate tables of arithmetic numbers such as logarithms. In the 1890 US census, Hollerith's punched card machines tabulated large amounts of data and, after its founding in 1924, IBM became wealthy from selling tabulating machines. In the 1920s engineers designed analog computers to calculate continuous functions by simulating them with circuits and gears. Designers of mechanical analog and digital computers were obviously computational thinkers. But even the analog computer idea is ancient, dating back to the Greek orrery, a mechanical device used to calculate planetary positions in 100 BCE.

Computing throughout the ages required computational thinking to design computational procedures and machines to automate them. The long quest for computing machines was driven not only by the need to speed up computation, but to eliminate human errors, which were common when easily bored or distracted humans performed many repetitive calculations. The designers believed automated machines would overcome the sources of error in calculations. Today we know better: while machines have eliminated some kinds of error, a whole horizon of new errors has appeared. Computing machines have become so complex that we do not know how much trust we can place on them.

Seeds of computational thinking advanced in sophistication over those many centuries. But only when the electronic computer became an industry in the 1950s did computer designers and programmers find an impetus to develop CT as a professional concern. These professionals gravitated to software because they could easily alter a machine's function by reprogramming the software. The emerging computing industry sought programmers and engineers schooled in computational thinking and practice. Educators inquired into how to teach them. The computer science (CS) field that emerged by 1960 inherited the responsibility for defining and teaching CT.

Throughout this book, we present many examples from the history of computing to illustrate the needs to which CT responded, the new possibilities for actions CT enabled, and the dramatic mind shifts CT caused in how we see automation, science, and the world. Although CT as a way of thinking has existed for thousands of years, the term "computational thinking" is relatively new: the first occurrence we are aware of is from 1980.

Emergence of Education Movement for CT in K–12 Schools

The first computer science (CS) department was founded at Purdue in 1962. Academic computer science matured along a bumpy and challenging path. Many universities were initially skeptical whether the new field was really new or scholarly enough; it looked rather like a branch of electrical engineering or applied mathematics. Many computer science departments were formed only after pitched political battles in their universities. Despite the political difficulties, the growth was steady. By 1980 there were about 120 CS departments in the US alone. Today all major and many smaller universities have one.

During the first 40 years, most of the concerns of practitioners in computing were focused on getting the technology to work. Everything we today consider a core technology had to be invented, designed, tested, and retested—take, for example, programming languages, operating systems, networks, graphics, databases, robotics, and artificial intelligence. One of the central elements of CT, designing reliable computing technologies, became a standard during those times.

In the 1980s, computing experienced a dramatic opening as scientists in all fields brought computation and computational thinking into mainstream science. At first, they used computation to simulate existing theoretical models or numerically tabulate and analyze data from experiments. But they soon discovered that thinking in terms of computation opened a door to a whole new way of organizing scientific investigation—CT led to Nobel Prizes for discoveries that had previously eluded scientists. Many declared computation a third pillar of science, alongside theory and experiment. CT was extended to designing computations throughout science, especially in response to "grand challenge" questions posed by leaders in the different fields. Every field of science eventually declared it had a computational branch, such as computational physics, bioinformatics, computational chemistry, digital humanities, or computational sociology.

Computer scientists had mixed reactions to these developments. Remembering their battle scars from forming departments, some were quite sensitive to the public image of computer science and wanted to control it. Some regarded the computational science movement as a means to hijack computer science by scientists who had previously expressed skepticism about computer science. As a result, computer scientists had a strong motivation to help the public understand the technology and theory of computing. Computer science educators worked with K–12 educators to define computer literacy courses, but these were not very popular. Around the year 2000 some educators proposed a more sophisticated approach they called "fluency with information technology"; high school teachers adopted a popular textbook in that area. Even with the success of the fluency approach, few high schools adopted a computer course. Computer science educators continued to seek ways to penetrate K–12 school systems and expose every student to computing.

A turning point came in 2006 when Jeannette Wing, then starting as an assistant director at the US National Science Foundation (NSF), reformulated the quest from fluency to computational thinking. She proposed that CT was a style of thinking that everyone needed to learn in the computing age. At the NSF she mobilized significant resources to train teachers, upgrade the Advanced Placement test, design new "CS principles" first-courses for colleges, define CT for the K–12 education sector, and issue curriculum recommendations for K–12 schools. This

"CS for all" movement has achieved much greater penetration of computing into K–12 schools than any of its predecessors.

The definitions of CT that have emerged from the post-2006 CT movement have moved conspicuously into the public view. But many public definitions, especially as interpreted to us by policymakers, are quite narrow compared to the notions of CT developed over the earlier centuries of computing. Mainstream media occasionally give a misinformed view of the scope and influence of computing. They have led people unfamiliar with computing to make inflated claims about the power of CT that will mislead students and others into making promises about computers they cannot deliver.

Our Objectives in This Book

Our objective in this book is to lay out the magnificent fullness of computational thinking and its precepts about computation and to dispel misunderstandings about the strengths and limits of computing.

Computational thinking evolved from ancient origins over 4,500 years ago to its present, highly developed, professional state. The long quest for computing machines throughout the ages was driven not only by the need to speed up computation, but also to eliminate human errors, which were common when easily bored or distracted humans performed many repetitive calculations. A special thinking skill evolved to accomplish this.

The development of computational thinking opened six important dimensions that are characteristic of CT today.

• *Methods*. Mathematicians and engineers developed methods for computing and reasoning that non-experts could put to work simply by following directions.

• *Machines*. Inventors looked for machines to automate computational procedures for the purpose of greater speed of calculation and reduction of human errors in carrying out computations. This led eventually to the invention of the digital electronic computer that harnesses the movement of electrons in circuits to carry out computations.

• *Computing Education*. University educators formed computer science to study and codify computation and its ways of thinking and practicing for institutions, businesses, science, and engineering.

• *Software Engineering*. Software developers formed software engineering to overcome rampant problems with errors and unreliability in software, especially large software systems such as major applications and operating systems.

• *Design*. Designers bring sensibilities and responsiveness to concerns, interests, practices, and history in user communities.

• *Computational Science*. Scientists formed computational science to bring computing into science, not only to support the traditions of theory and experiment, but also to offer revolutionary new ways of interpreting natural processes and conducting scientific investigations.

These six dimensions are like different windows looking at CT. Each window offers a particular angle of looking. Some aspects of CT may be visible through two windows, but each in a different light.

In the next six chapters we will examine CT in relation to each dimension above. We round out with a semifinal chapter on CT in modern general education and a concluding chapter about the future of CT.

Chapter 2: CT related to algorithmic procedures to automate processes

Chapter 3: CT related to computing machinery

Chapter 4: CT related to the theory of computing and academic discipline

Chapter 5: CT related to building large software systems

Chapter 6: CT related to designing for humans

Chapter 7: CT related to all the sciences

Chapter 8: Teaching CT for all

Chapter 9: The future of CT

We offer our stories of these dimensions to show you the power of CT and the ways in which it might help you in your work with computers and computation.

Computational thinking evolved from ancient origins over 4,500 years ago to its present, highly developed, professional state. The long quest for computing machines was driven not only by the need for speed, but also to eliminate human errors.

COMPUTATIONAL METHODS

If controversies were to arise, there would be no more need of disputation between two philosophers than between two accountants. For it would suffice to take their pencils in their hands, to sit down to their slates, and to say to each other (with a friend as witness if they liked): Let us calculate.

—Leibniz, in Russell's translation (1937)

When Peter was age 10, his twinkly-eyed math teacher told him he could read minds. "How could you do that?" Peter asked. The teacher said, "Here, I'll show you. Think of a number. Double it. Add 8. Divide by 2. Subtract your original number. Now concentrate hard on the answer. ... There, I see it. The answer is 4." Peter was so astonished he insisted that the teacher show him how to do this. "Well," said the teacher, "it's just math. Let's say X is your number.

Then I got you to calculate the expression $(2X+8) \div 2 - X = 4$. Your initial number was subtracted out. The answer is always half the number I told you to add." Peter had many fine moments reading the minds of his family and friends with this method. He also got hooked on mathematics and computing.

This is one of many mathematical methods handed down over many generations. Methods like this are behind a pack of "automatic tricks" used by magicians, where the trickster leads the subject through a series of steps to an answer known to the trickster and believed by the subject to be a secret. The sleights of mind to accomplish this are in the math steps known to the trickster but not the subject. They work for any trickster who follows the directions, even if the trickster has no idea why the directions work.

Many other methods with a more serious purpose were handed down through the ages. One of the earliest methods, taught to many schoolchildren today, comes from the Greek mathematician Euclid around 300 BCE. He gave a method to find the greatest common divisor (GCD) of two numbers, which is the largest integer that divides both numbers. Euclid found a clever reduction rule by noticing that the GCD of two numbers divides their difference. He repeatedly replaced the larger number with their difference, until both were the same. For example, $GCD(48,18) = GCD(30,18) = GCD(12,18) = GCD(12,6)$

= GCD(6,6) = 6. This method was used to reduce fractions. Today it is among the basic methods underlying cryptography.

Another famous method dating back to the Greeks was the Sieve of Eratosthenes, used to find all the prime numbers up to a limit. This method begins with a list of all the integers from 2 to the limit. It then crosses out all the multiples of 2, then all multiples of 3, then of 5, and so on. After each round of elimination, a new prime will be revealed; the next round crosses out all its multiples. This is a very efficient method to find small primes and has been adapted to finding large primes for keys in modern cryptographic systems.

The Greeks were also interested in calculating the areas of shapes. They did so by finding ways to tile the shapes with simple forms such as squares or triangles, and then successively reducing the dimensions of the forms until the original shape is almost completely filled with them. This method, first recorded in the period 400–350 BCE, was a precursor to better methods introduced in the modern calculus two thousand years later.

Many mathematicians used such methods to construct infinite series of simple terms that converged to some limit. Math books are filled with tables of series; mathematicians used them to replace long series with closed forms. One such example is the series $\frac{\pi}{4} = 1 - \frac{1}{3} + \frac{1}{5} - \frac{1}{7} + \frac{1}{9} - \ldots$, which gives a way to calculate the value of π, with greater precision when more terms are included.

The calculus, proposed independently by Newton and Leibniz around 1680, perfected the idea of approximating objects and curves by calculations over infinite series. The idea was to represent geometric forms and continuous curves with very small components that interacted locally—for example, fill the form with small boxes or model the curve as a series of tiny segments bound to their immediate neighbors with attractive forces. Then find a larger quantity such as area or length by adding the components. When the size of the components was allowed to approach zero, the expressions from these infinite sums would be exact. The rule of local interaction was represented as a derivative and the summation as an integral. Motivated by calculus, mathematicians evaluated functions by dividing time and space into small increments enumerated as a "grid" and iteratively calculated the value of a function at each grid point. This approach was a boon to physics, in which many mathematical models of physical phenomena were expressed as differential equations computable on finite grids.

Another famous mathematical method was the Gaussian elimination for solving systems of linear equations. Gauss worked with this method in the mid-1800s, although Chinese mathematicians knew it in 179 BCE. Very efficient forms of this algorithm are used in modern graphics displays to render three-dimensional objects in real time.

These few examples illustrate the richness and utility of the treasure trove of methods bequeathed to us over many centuries.

We can conclude from examining these methods that many were quite sophisticated. Their purpose was to capture, as a set of steps, what needed to be done in a complex calculation. Initially those steps were carried out by mathematicians, but with enough refinements a method could actually be used by anyone who could follow the directions. An important but subtle point is that the steps of the method had to be unambiguous. The less the ambiguity, the more trustworthy the method was in the hands of non-experts. It was a practice to reduce ambiguity by replacing fuzzy steps with precise chains of arithmetic and logic operations.

Beginning around 1650, some mathematicians started to look for machines to carry out the basic operations of common methods. Some methods were too complex to be easily remembered. Some methods needed to be iterated many times, and it was difficult for easily distracted human beings to complete them without errors. The machines would allow for much faster computation and fewer errors.

To build machines, mathematicians and inventors had to devise methods, such as the positioning of wheels and gears, to represent numbers with physical quantities. They also had to devise representations for logic steps such as a conditional jump or a loop. Today, representations of data and logic steps are important core elements of computational thinking. In the rest of this chapter we describe these aspects in more depth.

The Quest to Eliminate Intuition

The computational methods that evolved in the history of mathematics were intended to help builders, engineers, merchants, and scientists to calculate numbers. Ancient merchants invented number systems, accounting systems, and tools like the abacus to keep track of their businesses. Ancient engineers invented ways to build weapons of war and civilian structures of peace. All sought reliable methods of dealing with calculations involving large quantities of numbers so that their artifacts worked as intended and were dependable.

Their methods were handed down through apprenticeships and were worked mainly by experts. The experts developed rules-of-thumb, heuristics, learned hunches, and other intuitions that enabled them to solve problems that the uninitiated could not solve at all. The modern term "intuition" describes the expert's action of rapidly articulating a solution, based on extensive experience with similar situations. Intuition enables experts to find the essential core of the problem, skip unnecessary steps in solving it, and switch between solution approaches. Intuition is a manifestation of expertise and an enabler of new findings.

It might seem paradoxical then that throughout the ages much work in mathematics and logic has aimed at eliminating intuition from routine calculation and logical inference. Routine computing tasks were required to be as simple and "mechanical" as possible in order to always yield the same results regardless of who did the calculations. Mathematicians throughout history have sought to capture expertise into step-by-step procedures someone could follow with little training. Eliminating intuition from routine jobs did not mean eliminating experts, but rather making their expertise available to a large number of non-expert people.

The modern ideas of symbolic information representation, symbol processing, unambiguous computational steps, basic arithmetic, algorithms, synchronization of computations, and systematic error checking are all inheritances from those many centuries. By showing how mechanization of calculations has been a key feature in numerous developments of computational methods, our aim is to reveal how many computational thinking skills have been an integral part of many other kinds of thinking long before modern computing. Many features and practices of computational thinking support the designing of computations in many fields, not just in today's computer science.

Numerical Representations and Numerical Methods

Computational thinking, like much of modern science, relies on a process of *representing* things in the world in numbers or other symbols. A representation is an arrangement of symbols in an agreed format; each representation stands for something. We frequently use numbers to represent quantities such as census data on populations, business accounting ledgers, or engineering measurements. But numbers are not the only kinds of representation. Scientists and engineers represent phenomena with equations, such as a linear algebraic matrix for rotating an object or a differential equation for planetary motion. They also represent objects with mechanical artifacts such as models of buildings, wind tunnels, or planetary orreries. Numbers, equations, and models underpin the scientific ideals of measurement, experimentation, and reproducibility of results. In the computing age, representations with non-numeric symbols have become ubiquitous—for example, a Java language program, a bitmap of an image, or a soundtrack of music. Today we use the term *digitization* for the process of encoding almost any information

It might seem paradoxical that throughout the ages much work in mathematics and logic has aimed at eliminating intuition from routine calculation and logical inference. Eliminating intuition from routine jobs did not mean eliminating experts, but rather making their expertise available to a large number of non-expert people.

in the form of data representations that can be processed by computers.

Some skeptics did not trust these computational methods because numerical calculations were too susceptible to tiny errors in the precision of parameters and variables of the computation. This led the designers of methods to find constraints to keep accumulating errors within acceptable bounds. Today's computing machines have the same problems because the machines have limited precision (such as 32 or 64 bits) and round-off errors could accumulate in poorly designed algorithms. The calculus was a breakthrough because it allowed designers systematic ways to limit errors in their finite-difference calculations.

Decomposing Computing Tasks

During the time leading up to World War II, the US Army developed ever more sophisticated artillery that could fire shells over several miles. Gunners needed to know how to aim their artillery given the range, the difference of elevation, and the winds. The Army commissioned teams of human computers to work out firing tables for these guns. The gunners simply looked up the proper angle and direction to aim their guns, given their measurements of range, elevations, and winds.

One of the most well known of these teams comprised women working at Aberdeen Proving Grounds around 1940. They organized into assembly lines, each one doing a different stage of computation, until they compiled the firing tables. For tools they used mechanical calculators that do basic arithmetic (add, subtract, multiply, divide). They followed programs (i.e., sets of procedures) that managers established to divide the work and to govern which intermediate calculations moved from one human computer to the next. As trained mathematicians, the human computers were able to spot errors in their computations and thus keep the firing tables error free.

Today's computational thinking follows a similar pattern learned from those days:

• Break the entire computation into pieces that could be done by separate, interacting computers.

• Arrange the computers to optimize their communication and messaging patterns—for example into an assembly line or as a massive parallel fan-out and join.

• Include error checks into their methods so that recipients could verify that their inputs and outputs were correct.

Modern software designers are familiar with these principles under the following names: distributed computing, parallelization, and error checking. But those practices were not originally developed for machines—they were developed for human computers.

The US Army wanted to perform these computations at much larger scales and much faster than human teams could at Aberdeen, so it commissioned the electronic computer project ENIAC at University of Pennsylvania to do this. The designers of ENIAC faced huge challenges, such as learning how to build reliable electronic circuits to carry out the same computations much faster, and learning how to design the control programs and algorithms to prevent errors from accumulating in the computations. The method of decomposition of the task into unambiguous steps that passed data between them moved from being a management principle at Aberdeen into a design principle for automatic computers.

Concern over errors grew as machines became larger and more complex. Today in computer science we still teach this old wisdom: errors can happen at any stage of the computing process, including describing the problem, preparing the formulas, setting the constants, communicating data, recording and retrieving the data, carrying out the prescribed steps, or displaying the results.

Rules for Reasoning

Designing computations around unambiguous steps is not enough to give confidence that computations are free from errors. The steps must be strung together to follow a plan. At any stage in the computation the plan must tell us unambiguously what the next step is. Deciding what the next step is should be an exercise in logic.

A long-established branch of mathematics and philosophy has been concerned with logic. Can we provide the means to develop long chains of reasoning to solve problems and to verify that a given chain of reasoning is valid? As their counterparts in calculation, logicians sought ways to formalize and automate reasoning. Philosophers such as René Descartes and Gottfried Leibniz in the 1600s sought a language that would completely formalize human inference and reduce misunderstandings. Their goal was to establish a standard way to express concepts and rules of inference to definitively establish the truth or falsity of statements. According to their vision, such a "language of thought" would bring an end to disagreements in all domains, because every debate could be resolved through pure logic.

Progress toward this dream was slow. A breakthrough came in the 1800s. George Boole (1815–1864) was fascinated by how well-formulated, mathematical symbol systems were able to provide results for problems nearly automatically once the correct values were set in the formula.[1] In his book, *Laws of Thought* (1854), he presented "an algebra of thought" paralleling the algebra of numbers. His logic included variables whose values could be either *true* or *false*. He could form logical expressions, which were formulas of variables connected by operators such as *and*, *or*, and *not*. Nearly nine decades later (1937), Claude Shannon showed how Boole's algebra could describe the function of relay circuits in telephone systems and other electrical circuits. Boolean algebra was perfected for electronic circuit design in the 1950s, where it provided a means to find the smallest circuit for a given logic function and a means to design the circuit to avoid race conditions, which are ambiguous outputs caused by signals changing at different speeds in different parts of the circuit. Boolean algebra became a fixture of computer circuit design.

Despite its merits, Boole's algebra of logic had some serious limitations. Sentences that refer to sets, such as "everybody with a gray hair," while perfectly understandable in natural language, could not be expressed in Boolean logic. There was no way to generate a list of entities satisfying a formula; the concepts of "everybody" and "somebody" had no clear meaning. There were no rules for the important quantifiers *all* and *some*.

Gottlob Frege (1848–1925) presented a new system of logical inference, "language for pure thought" (1879), which today is called predicate logic. It included new quantifiers for *all* and *some* and closed gaps in Boolean logic. Frege's system also presented mechanical rules for symbol processing that could be followed without appealing to human intuition. Frege's predicate logic resembles a programming language in that it provides an artificial, formal language that presents unambiguous, deterministic, and mechanical rules for symbol processing.

In the early 1900s it looked like the vision for a formal language of thought was about to be fulfilled. The merger of mathematics and logic gave rise to Russell and Whitehead's magnum opus *Principia Mathematica* (1910) and to logical empiricism in the sciences. But one element was still missing to achieve the dream: a method for definitively deciding whether a statement in predicate logic was true or false. The question for whether such a method exists became known as the "decision problem." By the 1920s, it was taken as one of the major challenges in mathematics. Most mathematical logicians believed that a method existed, but no one could find it.

Mechanizing Computation

In 1935, a young Cambridge mathematics student was introduced to the decision problem. He became fascinated by the words a lecturer used to pose it: Was there a *mechanical* process for deciding, in a finite number of steps, whether a proposition in predicate logic is true or false? That student, Alan Turing (1912–1954), decided to develop a thoroughly mechanistic model of computing so that he could investigate the decision problem.

Turing started with the idea that, when calculating numbers, a human computer writes down a series of symbols on the paper. He represented the paper as a linear sequence of boxes each holding a single symbol. In calculating, the person moves attention from the current box to either of its nearest neighbors, possibly changing the symbol in the box. He assumed that the mind of the person doing the calculation was in one of a finite number of states, and that each of these basic moves on the paper was generated by a transition from the current state to a specified next state. This process continues until the calculation is complete. Turing took these basic actions—when in a given state, move left or right one box, read symbol at the current box, change the symbol in the current box, and move to the next state—as the basic mechanics of carrying out a computation. Clearly a machine could do these steps and keep track of the states. He noted that this machine modeled steps in calculating numbers or evaluating logic functions. After demonstrating how such a machine would work, Turing showed that there is one such machine that can simulate all others—implying that the machine model is a universal way to represent all calculations and proofs. He then proved that no machine could solve the decision problem because the very existence of a machine that could do so led to a logical paradox. This tour-de-force eventually made him famous for his "Turing machine" and its implications for computation.

A few years later, the electronic digital computer provided the means to *automate* calculation and proof— finally realizing, at least to some extent, the visions of mechanizing calculation and reasoning. Automation was the key to all these developments. To emphasize this, Turing called his machines *a-machines*, with "a" meaning "automatic." Similarly, the engineers designing the first electronic computers in the 1940s, such as UNIVAC and BINAC, gave them names ending in "-AC" meaning "automatic computer." Through the 1980s, computer science itself was often characterized as the science of automation. The key aspect of automation demands that a machine do the work without human intervention. The automatic computer is the ultimate realization of the old dream of making calculation available for the masses without requiring them to be experts in doing calculations.

Another key aspect of automation is recognizing that automatic computers cannot perform certain important tasks. Turing showed this when he proved no *a*-machine could exist to solve the decision problem. His same reasoning shows that problems of practical interest—such as determining whether a given computer program will halt or instead enter an infinite loop, or whether a given program contains a computer virus—cannot be solved by any machine. For this reason, a large segment of CT is concerned with how to provide partial solutions to problems that cannot be solved by automatic computers.

The automatic computer and the understandings of its limitations would not have been implemented without the merger of calculation and logic. It is no wonder many people consider logical thinking an essential element of computational thinking.

Computational Thinking Insights Come from Many Fields

It should be clear from this discussion of the origins of computational thinking that CT is not about how computer scientists think. Modern computer science is the last 1 percent of the historical timeline of computational thinking. Computer scientists inherited and then perfected computational thinking from a long line of mathematicians, natural philosophers, scientists, and engineers all interested in performing large calculations and complex inferences without error. CT is a feature of many fields, not only computing.

Logicians wished to create formal systems where one could start from the premises and, by following chains of substitutions within a formal system of rules, would always arrive at the same conclusions. The logical insights of Boole and Shannon—that a few logical operations can express the truth values of all propositional logic as well as the logical design of digital circuits—were driven by an old quest to banish all human emotion and judgment from logical inference. These insights are counted today as the first principles of computing. Frege's logical insight— predicate logic—presented a more powerful system of inference having many similarities with modern programming languages. Turing's insight into the essential features of automatic processing—that five actions and a finite number of states are enough for any computation— came from mathematical logic.

Other basic insights of computational thinking arose from science and engineering. Among the most important is the realization that most computations in science and technology require unimaginably long calculations that are well beyond the capabilities of a human team. The designers of computational methods to solve practical problems are obsessively concerned with controlling and limiting errors by making the computational steps simple and unambiguous and their connective logic unimpeachable.

The computer of today is the machine many sought throughout the ages to automate calculation and free it

The computer of today
is the machine many
sought throughout the
ages to automate
calculation and free it
from the frailties of
humans and the need
for their intervention
and judgment.

from the frailties of humans and the need for their intervention and judgment. Modern computing researchers and professionals embody this long history and excel at automating computations using the best methods available. However, as we will see in the next chapter, the wish of building real systems for very large, error-free computations has been exceedingly difficult to achieve.

COMPUTING MACHINES

The intolerable labour and fatiguing monotony of a continued repetition of similar arithmetical calculations, first excited the desire, and afterwards suggested the idea, of a machine, which, by the aid of gravity or any other moving power, should become a substitute for one of the lowest operations of human intellect.

—Charles Babbage (July 3, 1822, letter to Humphry Davy)

Now we will look at the evolution of computing machines and the dimension of computational thinking needed to design and understand them. The primary practical motivation for building computing machines was always to speed up computation and eliminate the errors inherent in human computing.

People have always been fascinated by the idea of building devices that automated aspects of human behavior or human thinking. For millennia, craftsmen built automata for art and amusement, such as animated animal figures, music boxes, player pianos, and human-like figurines mimicking people's behavior. The Mechanical Turk, a chess-playing automaton, created a sensation in 1770 because it seemed to mechanize chess play, then considered a high-order mental skill. It was later revealed to be an elaborate hoax. But it titillated the curiosity of inventors who wondered if they could really build a chess-playing machine. Some philosophers believed that automata for calculation, another revered human mental skill, might be more feasible because the rules of basic arithmetic were much clearer and simpler than the rules and strategies of chess.

The Rise of Computing Machines

When experts can codify, as procedural steps, what they know about calculation and reasoning, their knowledge becomes useful to many non-experts, who can obtain the results without error simply by following directions. But no matter how precise the procedure, human operators are prone to making mistakes. They are forgetful, they do not fully understand every computational operation, they are easily distracted, and they are quickly bored by a long routine calculation. No matter how simple and unambiguous the steps, human computers make mistakes. A lot of them. One study of 40 volumes of old mathematical tables found 3,700 errors, and another found 40 errors on just one page.

For this reason, inventors through the ages sought computing machines and aids for calculation that would allow humans to complete longer computations with fewer errors. This was a slow process. The slide rule was invented around 1620. By sliding sticks marked with logarithmic scales past each other, it implemented the method of multiplication based on summing logarithms. But the slide rule could not add or subtract. Blaise Pascal designed a calculator in 1642; it could add and subtract, but could not multiply or divide. Attempts by others to extend Pascal's design to permit multiplication failed.

The slide rule found its home among engineers and the arithmetic calculator among mathematicians and accountants. Over the following centuries, these kinds of machines were gradually improved. By the 1930s, Keuffel and Esser Company was the primary supplier of log-trig slide rules and Marchant was the primary supplier of mechanical calculators that did all four arithmetic operations. Many slide-rule and mechanical calculator companies were swept away by the avalanche of change unleashed by the electronic computer revolution in the 1950s. New companies such as Hewlett-Packard and Texas Instruments started to produce all-electronic desktop calculators that could perform all slide-rule and arithmetic functions. The coup de grâce came in 1972 with the HP-35 programmable handheld calculator, which replaced the slide-rule on the engineer's belt.

Despite their popularity, the slide rule and calculating machine had two serious limitations. First, they could not perform long chains of calculations; human operators had to do that. Second, these tools could only be used for a single purpose. The electronic digital computer overcame these limitations with a radical idea: software stored internally in the machine's memory. Software could perform long calculations and could easily be adjusted to change the operation of the underlying machine.

Precursors to the idea of software originated well before the electronic computing age. In the early 1700s, French textile weavers experimented with machines that could weave complex patterns using an automatic loom. One of the more well known of these machines was the Jacquard loom, which was controlled by long chains of punched cards; a hole in a card let a hook through, lifting a thread that became part of a single line of the weave. Jacquard's automatic loom revolutionized textile weaving. Jacquard's cards were a form of external, changeable software that controlled the operation of the loom.

The idea of controlling machines with punched cards appealed to Herman Hollerith, who designed a machine to tabulate the data from the 1890 US Census. He recorded each citizen's data as a pattern of holes punched in a card, representing characteristics such as sex, address, and ethnic origin. The tabulating machine selected out cards meeting given characteristics and tallied statistics for the selected group of citizens. With Hollerith's machine, the Census Bureau completed its analysis of 63 million records in one year, far faster and cheaper than any previous census. In the following years, the same technology was adopted for myriad data processing tasks: keeping track of health of tens of thousands of soldiers, agricultural censuses, rail freight waybills, and so on.

Before seeing where tabulating machines led, we would like to back up 50 years to the significant development by Charles Babbage and Ada Lovelace: the general-purpose computer.

The Babbage Machines

Charles Babbage designed two significant computing machines in his long career. His Difference Engine (ca. 1820) automated the calculation of mathematical tables such as tables of logarithms or sines. His Analytical Engine (ca. 1840) was a general-purpose computer capable of any computable function.

In Babbage's day, experts prepared books of tables of important functions such as the logarithms of all six-digit numbers. These tables were commonly used for mathematical calculations; for example, one could multiply two numbers by looking up and adding their logarithms. These tables were computed by hand using difference formulas that calculated each line of the table from the previous line. Babbage knew that these hand-computed books contained many errors, and those errors sometimes led to serious consequences. For example, he argued that errors in the navigation tables used by the British Navy caused shipwrecks. He wished to eliminate the errors by replacing humans with machinery that does not get tired, bored, or distracted. He conceived of a machine that he called Difference Engine to calculate and print tables of numbers. Intrigued, the British government gave him funds to develop it.

Babbage spent the better part of the next 20 years trying to build his machine. It was a much bigger challenge than he thought: the mechanical engineering methods of the day were not able to produce thousands of gears and levers with the precision needed to avoid skipping or jamming. In the 1830s he conceived of a new design called the Analytical Engine, which would need fewer parts and would be more powerful—capable of calculating *any* mathematical function. But by that time, the government distrusted him over his failure to deliver a Difference Engine and refused to back his Analytical Engine project. He pursued that project with scraps of funding until his death in 1871, but never completed it. His visionary ideas lay dormant for the next 80 years.

The Analytical Engine took instructions from punched cards, an idea from Jacquard's loom. The punched cards contained a program that would instruct the machine to automatically compute a mathematical function. It was able to decide what to do based on earlier results (selection) and repeat parts of its program (looping). It had separate units for separate functions of the machine: input, processing, memory, and output. It composed machine instructions from microprograms.

Babbage collaborated with a gifted English mathematician, Ada Lovelace, who designed algorithms for the Analytical Engine. One of her example programs calculated a sequence of rational numbers called Bernoulli numbers. Babbage and Lovelace are often regarded as the first programmers. What is more, Lovelace saw Babbage's machine as more than a number calculator; for her it was a processor of any information that can be encoded in symbols. She called the study of such programs "the science of operations." Her insight that computing machines can calculate not only over numbers, but over symbols that can stand for anything in the world, anticipated by a hundred years a key tenet of the modern computer age. Lovelace saw the computer as an information machine.

The vision of both Babbage and Lovelace was groundbreaking. Their designs introduced many ideas today considered as features that distinguish computational thinking from other kinds of thinking. Besides representing programs in a changeable external medium, the Analytical Engine embodied many aspects of modern computers: digital representation of data, programming, machine-executable algorithms, control structures for choosing cases and looping, arithmetic-logic unit, and microprogramming to break machine instructions into low-level logic gate operations. Ironically, some central insights of the computer age were born in the age of steam.

The Stored-Program Computer

Babbage's logical designs for his computer could not be realized on the era's technology, but many decades later, the dawning age of electronics opened up new possibilities. The period from the late 1930s was one of intense experimentation to build computing machines. Konrad Zuse built a computer in Germany in 1938, but the German government did not take it seriously and it made little impact. Howard Aiken, in partnership with IBM and sponsored by the US Navy, built the Mark I at Harvard in 1944. It was an electromechanical computer that straddled the mechanical world governed by Newton's laws of motion and the light-speed world governed by Maxwell's laws of electromagnetism. Its programs and input data were stored externally on punched paper tapes.

At the Moore School of Electrical Engineering at the University of Pennsylvania, John Mauchly and Presper Eckert—with support from the US Army—designed what is perhaps the most famous among the first electronic computers. Their ENIAC machine went into operation in 1945 and was used to calculate artillery-firing tables and explore the feasibility of the thermonuclear weapon. The ENIAC (Electronic Numerical Integrator and Computer) took its program from an external wire patch board; programming it was tedious. The ENIAC machine was very influential as a proof-of-concept of fully electronic computing: it worked, it was fast, and it inspired better machines soon after. Its engineers founded Univac, the first commercial company to offer an electronic computer.

In 1945, the ENIAC team, joined by John von Neumann, met to design a better machine based on their experience. Aside from the ENIAC being difficult to program, its memory was limited, and it used many thousands of vacuum tubes (18,000 of them) that gradually wore out. For their new design, the team separated the machine into three main subsystems: the central processing unit

(CPU) for performing the arithmetic and logical operations, the memory for storage, and the input-output (I/O) unit for communicating with the external world. To speed up the computer, they designed a CPU that took its instructions from memory, not external punched cards or tapes, thus initiating the "stored program computer" idea. By a quirk of history, this way of organizing a machine became known as the "von Neumann architecture" because von Neumann took the notes on their meetings and distributed them. He claimed to be the note taker, not the designer. The von Neumann architecture emerged as a consensus, the plan for almost all commercial computers from that time to the present. The notion that a CPU traces out an instruction sequence among instructions stored in memory has become a central tenet of computational thinking.

Computational Thinking and Machines

Let us now examine the various precepts of computational thinking that these early machines and their operating systems gave us.

Digital Representations with Signals and Binary Codes
To be processable, data must be represented as signals in the machine or as measurable disturbances in the structure

of storage media. There is no information without representation. Arithmetic operations such as add and subtract must be represented as rules for transforming signals. One early way to represent a decimal digit was a ring of 10 dual-triode vacuum tubes simulating a 10-position wheel. This scheme was much more expensive than a 4-tube binary representation of the same digit. Proposals to represent decimal digits with 10 distinct voltages were dismissed because of the complexity of the circuits. Engineers quickly settled on using binary codes to represent numbers because binary-coded arithmetic used many fewer components than decimal-coded arithmetic, and because circuits to distinguish two voltage values were much more reliable than circuits to distinguish more than two values. Moreover, storage could easily be built from available two-state technology such as acoustic delay lines, magnetic cores, flip-flop circuits, or phosphor patches on a cathode-ray screen. The decision to abandon decimal arithmetic and use binary codes for everything in the computer led to very simple, much more reliable circuits and storage media. The term "bit" came into standard use as shorthand for "binary digit." Today no one can think about contemporary computers without thinking about binary representations.

It is important to keep in mind that internally the computer does not process numbers and symbols. Computer circuits deal only with voltages, currents, switches, and malleable materials. The patterns of zeroes and ones are abstractions invented by the designers to describe what their circuits do. Because not every binary code is a valid description of a circuit, symbol, or number, the designers invented syntax rules that distinguished valid codes from invalid ones. Although the machine cannot understand what patterns mean, it can distinguish allowable patterns from others by applying the syntax rules.

We cannot overemphasize the importance of physical forms in computers—such as signals in circuits or magnetic patches on disks—for without these physical effects we could not build a computer. Although computer programs appear to be abstractions, they cannot work without the machines harnessing physical phenomena to represent and process binary numbers. For this reason, it is safe to say that every dataset, every program, and every logic circuit layout is a "strategic arrangement of stuff."

Boolean Algebra and Circuit Design

Because of Claude Shannon's insight that George Boole's logic precisely described electronic switching circuits, today we cannot think about computers without thinking about Boolean algebra. Boolean algebra helps us understand how the hardware implements the machine instructions generated by a compiler. But Boolean algebra is an abstraction. Sometimes it hides physical race conditions caused by multiple signals following different paths to the same output; race conditions can cause errors by causing the circuits to deviate from their Boolean formulas. This confounds programmers who are only aware of the abstractions and not the circuitry, and for that reason cannot find the errors by studying their programs.

The Clocked CPU Cycle for Basic Computational Steps

The physical structure of computers consists of registers, which store bit patterns, and logic circuits, which compute functions of the data in the registers. It takes time for these logic circuits to propagate signals from their input registers to their output registers. If new inputs are provided before the circuits settle, the outputs are likely to be misinterpreted by subsequent circuits. Engineers solved this problem by adding clocks to computers. At each clock tick the output of a logic circuit is stored in its registers. The interval between ticks is long enough to guarantee that the circuit is completely settled before its output is stored. Computers of the von Neumann architecture cannot function without a clock. Today computers are rated by their clock speeds—for example, a "3.8 GHz processor" is one whose clock ticks 3.8 billion times a second.

The existence of clocks gives a precise physical interpretation to the "algorithmic steps" in the digital realm. Every algorithmic step must be completed before the next step is attempted. The machine supports this by guaranteeing each instruction will be correctly finished before the next instruction is attempted. (There are a few types of computers that do not use clocks, but they will not be discussed here.) Clocks are essential to support our notion of computational steps and guarantee that the computer performs them reliably.

Control Flow

From the time of Babbage and Lovelace, programmers have realized that the machine must be able to decide which instructions are next. They do not always follow a linear sequence. In the von Neumann architecture, the address of the next instruction is stored in a CPU register called the program counter (PC), which is updated after each instruction. The default is to execute the next instruction in sequence (PC set to PC+1). One common deviation from linearity is to branch to another instruction at a different memory location, say X. The decision to branch is governed by a condition C (such as "is A equal to B?") and the jump from one part of the program to another part is implemented by an instruction that says "if C then set PC to X." This method of controlling the program counter so that the program execution jumps to a different part of the code is manifested in computational thinking as the *if-then-else* construct in programming languages.

Loops: Small Programs Making Big Computations

If all our programs were nothing more than decision trees of instruction sequences each selected by *if-then-else*, they could never generate computations longer than the number of instructions in the program. The loop allows us to design computations that are much longer than the size of the program. A loop is a sequence of instructions that are repeated over and over until a stopping condition is satisfied. A loop can be implemented with an *if-then-else* that branches back to the loop's start when the stopping condition is false. A common programming error is a faulty stopping condition that does not exit the loop. That behavior is called an "infinite loop."

Alan Turing proved that there is no algorithm for inspecting a program to determine if any of its loops is infinite. This makes debugging a challenging problem that cannot be automated. Programmers spend a great deal of time looking for mistakes in their programs.

Some programs are built on purpose to loop forever. This is very common in service processes on the Web. The service process waits at a homing position for an incoming request; it then executes code to fulfill the request and returns to its homing position. While this facilitates designing service processes, it does not remove the challenge of proving that the service process always returns to its homing position.

The Address-Contents Distinction

Stored-program computing machines introduced a distinction between an address (a name) and a value (associated with the name). In a program, a variable X names a memory location holding a value. In classical algebra, X is an unknown value. In a program, the statement "X=3" means "store the value 3 in the memory location named X." Contrast this with the meaning of "X=3" in classical algebra, which is "the unknown X has the value 3." In a program, "X=3" is a command; in algebra it is a fact. This distinction is part of our computational thinking. Novice programmers who do not make this distinction often draft programs that do not work.

Subprograms

By the late 1940s, designers of computers realized that a common practice of programmers would be to write code for standard functions that could be invoked from anywhere in their programs. For example, an expert programmer could write code for a SORT function that anybody else can use to arrange a list of numbers in ascending order. To enable the efficient invocation of such subprograms, the designers included a new kind of branch instruction in their machines. An instruction "CALL X" would remember the current value of the program counter (PC) and then set PC to X, thereby transferring control to the subprogram stored in memory at location X. On completion, the subprogram would execute a "RETURN" instruction that restored the remembered PC value, enabling the original program to resume operation from the point of call.

The idea of subprograms has become an important principle of computational thinking. Hardware designers have given us efficient implementations. Subprograms appear in programming languages as "subroutines," "functions," and "procedures." It is taken for granted today that programs are divided into modules implemented as subprograms.

Universal Machines

In 1936, Alan Turing introduced the idea of a universal machine—a computer that could simulate any other computer, given the program of the other computer. The universal machine itself was not very complicated. This idea was implicit in the designs of machines dating back to Babbage's Analytical Engine: designers build one base machine that can run many programs. The base machine is an example of a universal machine. Today this is taken for granted: software designers assume that compilers and operating systems will make their software work on a basic underlying universal machine.

Sometimes people equate the idea of a universal machine with a stored program computer. They are not the same. Babbage's Analytical Engine was a universal machine whose programs were external decks of punched cards. The ENIAC was a universal machine whose programs were external patch boards. After 1945, computers were universal machines that stored their programs in internal memory.

The stored program computer makes it possible to switch the interpretation of a set of bits in memory between data and instruction. The very same patterns in the computer memory can be bits that represent things (data), as well as bits that do things (instructions). A compiler, for example, generates machine code as output data; the CPU can immediately interpret those data as executable instructions. Some early machines allowed programs to modify their own code to achieve greater efficiency. But most operating systems prohibited this by making machine code read-only: that allows the sharing but not the changing of code. The older idea of self-modifying programs is far from dead: malware today constantly modifies its own code to escape detection by antivirus software.

Fault Tolerance and Data Protection

Logic circuits regularly experience errors from physical causes. For example, the state of a component might be unpredictable if conflicting signals arrive at the same time, or if the clock is too fast to allow some components to settle into new states, or if components deteriorate and fail over time. Circuit engineers spend a lot of time on fault tolerance. They have generally done a good job because hardware is sufficiently reliable that users do not worry about errors in the hardware.

In the 1950s design engineers began to think about multiple-access computers that would be shared within a user community. Correspondingly, CT expanded from single-user computations to multi-user computations. Multi-user systems had to guarantee that no user could access another's data without explicit permission. This setup would provide the significant benefit of allowing users to share programs and data and would reduce the cost per user by spreading costs across many users. Designers of the first operating systems achieved this by isolating each executing program in a private region of memory defined by a base address and length. The base-length numbers were placed in a CPU register so that all memory accesses from the CPU were confined to the defined region of memory. This idea of partitioning memory and setting up the hardware so that it was impossible for a CPU to access outside its private memory was crucial for data protection. It not only protected user programs from each other; it could be used to protect users from untrusted software, which could be confined into its own memory region.

Users of machines and networks today are aware they are sharing their machines and networks with many others. They assume that the operating systems and networks are enforcing the isolation principle by keeping the executing programs in private memory regions. When they download new software they do not trust, they expect their operating system to isolate the new software in a memory region called a "sandbox."

Although it has been in our computational thinking for a long time that operating systems isolate programs, many computer chips designed in the 1980s dropped out the memory bound checks in order to achieve greater speed. Many security specialists are now regretting this omission. New generations of hardware may once again enforce the security checks that CT experience leads users to believe are present.

Beyond the von Neumann Architecture

One of the popular modern definitions of computational thinking is "formulating problems so that their solutions can be expressed as computational steps carried out by a machine." This definition is closely tied to the framework of the von Neumann architecture. In effect, the definition is a generalization of the operation of the CPU in a von Neumann machine.

After half a century, the von Neumann architecture has been approaching its limits. There are two main reasons. One is that the underlying chip technology, which has been doubling its component count every two years according to Moore's law, can no longer absorb the continuous reductions in component size. Soon components will be so small they cannot comprise enough atoms to allow them to function properly. The impending end of Moore's law has motivated extensive research into alternative architectures.

The other reason is that the separation of processor and memory in von Neumann architecture creates massive data traffic between processor and memory. One technology invented to lessen the processor-memory bottleneck is the cache, which retains data in the CPU rather than returning it to memory. Another technology intersperses processor and memory in a cellular array to spread the data load among many smaller processor-memory channels. A third technology is special purpose chips—ones that do a particular job exceptionally well but are not general-purpose computers themselves. An example is the graphics processing units (GPUs) now permeating every computer with a graphics display. Special purpose processors are themselves the subject of extensive research.

Two new categories of computer architecture have been getting special attention. Both are potential disruptors of today's computational thinking. One is the neural network, which has been the powerhouse behind recent advances in artificial intelligence. A neural network maps large bit patterns (for example, the bits of a photograph) into other bit patterns (for example, labeled faces in the

The invention of the fully-electronic stored program computer changed the very concept of computing and created a fresh world of computational concepts that had few counterparts or precursors. The concepts, practices, and skills for designing programs and computers quickly diverged from mathematics and logic. It was a profound change.

photograph). The input signals travel through multiple layers where they are combined according to assigned weights. An external algorithm trains the network by presenting it with a large number of input-output pairs and assigning the internal weights so that the network properly maps each input to its corresponding output. Training a network is computationally intensive, taking anywhere from many hours to several days. A trained network is very fast, giving its output almost instantly after the input is presented. Graphics-processing chips have been successful in achieving fast response of a trained neural network. Although machines capable of only pattern matching and recognition are not general-purpose (universal) computers, they have produced amazing advances in automating some human cognitive tasks, such as recognizing faces. However, there is no mechanism for verifying that a neural network will give the proper output when presented with an input not in its training set. It is very jarring to our computational thinking to be unable to "explain" how a computational network generated its conclusion.

The other computer architecture getting special attention uses quantum mechanical effects to process data. These quantum machines represent bits with electron spins and connections with quantum effects such as entanglement. Quantum computers can perform some computations much faster than von Neumann computers.

One such computation is factoring a large composite number into its two constituent primes. The intractability of factoring on von Neumann architectures has been the principle behind the security of the RSA cryptosystem, which is currently the most secure cryptosystem in wide use. Quantum computers threaten to break its security. Because their operation is nothing at all like that of the von Neumann computers, most people trained in computer science rather than physics find it very difficult to understand the operation of these machines or how to program them.

These two examples illustrate how each kind of machine has an associated style of computational thinking and is quite good at particular kinds of problems. A person with advanced knowledge in CT would be familiar with these architectures and, as part of the design process, would select the best architecture for solving the problem. At the same time, particular machine types can also induce a kind of "blindness"—for example, designers schooled in the basic von Neumann architecture think in terms of instructions and have trouble understanding how a quantum computer works.

Until the 1940s, computing was seen largely as an intellectual task of humans and a branch of mathematics and logic. The invention of the fully electronic stored program computer changed the very concept of computing, and it created a fresh world of computational concepts that had few counterparts or precursors. The concepts, practices, and skills for designing programs and computers quickly diverged from mathematics and logic. It was a profound change.

And until the 1940s, computational thinking was embedded in the tacit knowledge and state-of-the-art practices of many different fields, including mathematics, logic, engineering, and natural sciences. After the 1940s, computational thinking started to become the centerpiece of the new profession that designed information machines to do jobs humans never thought were possible.

COMPUTER SCIENCE

The question "What can be automated?" is one of the most inspiring philosophical and practical questions of contemporary civilization.

—George Forsythe (1969)

In the 1950s academics started to advocate for the formation of computer science programs in universities to meet a rising hunger for learning the new technology. Many precepts of CT were refined and perfected in computer science departments since that time. We turn now to the story of how CT developed in the universities.

Before we begin, we would like to point out a few key aspects of the academic environment in which CT developed. First and foremost, computing is a technical field blending engineering, science, and mathematics. Most computing students come to university to learn a profession of software and hardware designers, not to obtain a general education. Employers also come to university to recruit graduates for jobs. Thus, the CT that evolved along with academic computing has always had a strong component around design and has been strongly influenced by what employers say they need.

But that is not all. Universities are organized into a set of departments by discipline and a scattering of cross-disciplinary institutes and centers. The departments fiercely protect their identities, budgets, and space. Because their budgets depend on students enrolled, they are protective of their enrollments. And because enrollments depend on reputation and reputation on research productivity, university departments are protective of their research domains.

Another important shaping aspect of academia is the practice of seeking consensus on all decisions. Everybody wants a say, whether it is hiring a new person, awarding tenure, deciding what courses will be offered, approving possibly overlapping courses proposed by other departments, or approving the formation of new programs or departments.

This is the atmosphere in which new CS departments and academic computational thinking were formed. The founders worried about curriculum and industry demand in the context of a set of consensus-seeking departments fiercely guarding their prerogatives, always concerned with public image and identities.

The new departments proposed by the founders were split off from their existing departments. Their home departments often did not support the split because they would lose students, budget, and identity. The founders encountered a lot of resistance from other departments that did not deem a new department focused on computer technology to be legitimately science or engineering, or see that it would provide a unique intellectual perspective. Forging a consensus favoring formation of a new department was a challenge. Thus, the founders spent a good deal of time debating about the substance of computing, why it was different and new, and how it would benefit the other fields. They built a good case and were successful. Slowly the number of computer science departments grew, from 1 in 1962 to around 120 in 1980 in the US alone. Eventually in the late 1990s computer science took off as people finally realized the computing revolution is real. Today nearly every university has a computer science department.

Computer science departments are found in schools of science, engineering, and even business. Why so many homes? The answer echoes those early political fights: the new departments were established in the schools that were most welcoming. Because most of the departments were in schools of science and engineering, by the 1980s, computer scientists were labeling their field "CS&E." That mouthful was simplified in the 1990s as "computing" became a popular shorthand for CS&E and its European counterpart "informatics." In the 1990s some universities went further and established separate schools of computing, a movement that continues to grow today. What a turnaround!

Two academic computer societies were formed in the early days: the IEEE-CS (Institute of Electrical and Electronics Engineers Computer Society) in 1946, and the ACM (Association for Computing Machinery) in 1947. Because of their diligence to develop and promote curriculum recommendations, there are a series of snapshots of the computing curriculum at regular intervals—1968, 1978, 1989, 1991, 2001, and 2013. These snapshots show how the concerted efforts of computing pioneers to articulate a unique identity for computer science led them to recognize computational thinking as a distinguishing aspect from the beginning. In hindsight, we can discern four eras describing how universities thought about computing and how those views of computational thinking changed:

Phenomena surrounding computers (1950s–1970s)

Programming as art and science (1970s)

Computing as automation (1980s)

Computing as pervasive information processes (1990s to present)

We will discuss these eras in following sections.

These four stages of CT development in the universities were strongly shaped by the initial resistance to computer science from other fields: academic computer scientists spent a lot of effort clarifying and justifying their field. But computer science was not always the receiver of resistance. There were two important instances when computer science was the giver. One was the computational science movement in the 1980s, which was eschewed by many computer scientists. A common reaction to an announcement by the physics or biology department that they were setting up a computational science branch would be a howl of protest that those departments were impinging on the territory of computing. Some computer scientists believed that physics and biology, having now recognized the importance of computing, were trying to hijack the field they once vociferously opposed. Eventually computer scientists got over this and now work collaboratively with computational sciences. We will talk about computational science in chapter 7.

A similar process happened with software engineering. The computing departments that viewed themselves as science were not receptive to the practices of teaching and doing projects common in engineering. Software engineering had trouble gaining a foothold in those departments. There was an ongoing debate in computer science for a long time about whether software engineering is part of computer science or should be its own department. We will talk about that in chapter 5.

Phenomena Surrounding Computers

The developers of early automatic computers realized quickly that the new machines required a way of thinking and designing that differed from anything already existing in science or engineering. The ACM and IEEE started journals for the young field in the early 1950s. The Moore School, home of the ENIAC project, was an early starter of computing education in 1946 with a two-month intensive course on "theory and techniques for design of electronic digital computers." In the 1950s the Moore School offered a multi-discipline degree in computing that included numerical analysis, programming, and programming language design. Other schools started their own programs.

These early efforts to establish computing as an academic discipline were slow to gain traction. The impediment was more than a cautionary hesitancy to see if computers were here to stay; it was a deep doubt about whether computing had academic substance beyond mathematics, electrical engineering, and physics. Outsiders typically saw the computing field of the 1950s as an impenetrable and anarchistic thicket of idiosyncratic technology tricks. What is more, the different perspectives to thinking about computing were disunited: those who designed computing machines were mostly unaware of important developments in the theory of computing such as Turing on computable numbers, Church on lambda calculus, Post on string manipulation, Kleene on regular expressions, Rabin and Scott on nondeterministic machines, and Chomsky on the relation between grammars and classes of automata.[1]

Academics who proposed full-fledged computer science departments or programs in research universities met stiff resistance. Many critics did not believe in the value of computing's new ways: common objections included lack of unique intellectual content and lack of adequate theoretical basis. Purists argued that computers were human-made artifacts and not natural occurrences, and thus their study could not be counted among the noble natural sciences. On top of all that, many doubted whether computing would last. Until there was a consensus among many departments, no one could found a computer science department.

This tide began to change in 1962, when Purdue established the first computer science department and Stanford followed soon thereafter. Over the next two decades the number of departments grew slowly but steadily to well over a hundred just in the US. Even so, many academics continued to question whether computer science was a legitimate field of science or engineering.

A major shift in the question about the legitimacy of computing happened in 1967, when three well-recognized computer scientists—Allen Newell, Alan Perlis, and Herbert Simon—published a famous letter in *Science* addressing the question. They wrote: "Wherever there are phenomena, there can be a science to describe and explain those phenomena. Thus, ... botany is the study of plants, ... zoology is the study of animals, astronomy the study of stars, and so on. Phenomena breed sciences. ... There are computers. Ergo, computer science is the study of computers. The phenomena surrounding computers are varied, complex, rich."[2] From this basis they quickly dismissed six objections, including the one that computers are human-made and are therefore not legitimate objects of a science. Herb Simon, a Nobel laureate in economics, so objected to the notion that there could be no science surrounding human-made objects that he wrote a now-classic book titled *Sciences of the Artificial* refuting this idea.[3] He gave an example from time-sharing systems (computers that allow many simultaneous users):

The early development of time-sharing systems could not have been guided by theory as there was none, and most predictions about how time-sharing systems would behave were astonishingly inaccurate. It was not possible to develop a theory of time-sharing systems without actually building those systems; after they were built, empirical research on their behavior led to a rich theoretical base about them. In other words, CT could not approach problems from one direction only—the engineering aspects and scientific-mathematical aspects of computing evolved in a synergistic way to yield a science that was not purely a natural science.

The notion of computing as the study of phenomena surrounding computers quickly gained traction, and by the end of the 1960s was taken as the definition of computing. A view of the field's uniqueness started to form around that notion. The term "algorithmic thinking" was used to describe the most obvious aspect of new kind of thinking. The field's unique aims, typical problems, methods of solving those problems, and kinds of solutions were the basis of CT.

The computing pioneers expanded computational thinking beyond what they inherited from the long history of computation. They focused on the construction principles of programs, computing machines, and operating systems. They worked out a large number of computing concepts that are today taken for granted, including named variables, control structures, data structures, data types, formal programming languages, subroutines, compilers, input-output protocols, instruction pipelines, interrupt systems, computing processes, memory hierarchies, caches, virtual memory, peripherals, and interfaces. Programming methodology and computer systems architecture were main drivers in the development of computational thinking. By 1970, most computer scientists said that computing's characteristic ways of thinking and practicing—which today are called computational thinking—embrace all the knowledge and skills relating to computers.

Computational thinking divided early into a hardware flavor and a software flavor. The hardware flavor was followed by computer engineers in the engineering school; the software flavor by software designers and computing theorists in the science school.

Programming as Art and Science

The 1960s were a maturing period for computing that produced considerable richness in the ways computer scientists thought about their work and their field. The subfield of operating systems was born in the early 1960s to bring cheap, interactive computing to large user communities—CT acquired a systems attitude. The subfield of software engineering was born in the late 1960s from a concern that existing models of programming were incapable of developing reliable and dependable production software—CT acquired an engineering attitude. The subfield of networking was born in 1967 when the AR-PANET project was started—CT acquired a networking attitude.

With a solid, reliable technology base in place, the field's attention shifted to programs and programming. Many programming languages came into existence along with standard ways of programming. A huge interest in formal verification of programs welled up, seeking a theory-based way to demonstrate that programs were reliable and correct. A similar interest in computational complexity also welled up, seeking analytical ways to assess just how much computational work the different algorithms required.

Computer programs are expressions of algorithms in a formal language that, when compiled to machine-executable form, control the actions of a machine. Programs are central to nearly all of computing: Most professionals and researchers in computing work in some way or another with programs. On the first stored-program computers of the 1940s, programming was done in assembly languages that converted short abbreviated codes for instructions line-by-line to machine code that computers can run. For example, the instruction "ADD R1,R2,R3" would place the sum of registers R1 and R2 into register R3. That instruction was converted to machine code by substituting binary codes for ADD, R1, R2, and R3. Writing programs in assembly language was very tedious and error-prone.

Programming languages were invented to provide precise higher-level expressions of what the programmer wanted, which could then be unambiguously translated by a compiler to machine code. This greatly simplified the job of programming, making it much more productive and much less error-prone. The first widely adopted programming languages introduced a plethora of new CT concepts that had few or no counterparts in other intellectual traditions.

Most programming languages were aimed at helping automate important jobs such as analyzing scientific data and evaluating mathematical models (FORTRAN in 1957), making logical deductions (LISP in 1958), or tracking business inventories and maintaining customer databases (COBOL in 1959). A few languages aimed at allowing people to communicate precise specifications of algorithms that could be incorporated into other languages. The ALGOL language (1958) was developed from this perspective.

The idea that languages cater to particular ways of thinking about problems came to be called "programming paradigms." For example, imperative programming saw programs as series of modules (called "procedures") whose instructions commanded the machine. FORTRAN, COBOL, and ALGOL all fit this category. Object-oriented programming treated programs as collections of relatively self-sufficient units, "objects," that interact with each other and with the outside world by exchanging messages. Later languages such as Smalltalk and Java fit this category. Functional programming treated programs as sets of mathematical functions that generate output data from input data. LISP is an example.

These programming paradigms were seen in the 1970s as different styles of algorithmic thinking. They all sought programs that are clear expressions for humans to read and perform correctly and efficiently when compiled and executed. Donald Knuth, in his major works *The Art of Computer Programming* and *Literate Programming,* and Edsger Dijkstra in his work on structured programming, epitomized the idea that computing is about algorithms in this sense. By 1980, most computer scientists said that computational thinking is a set of skills and knowledge related to algorithms and software development.

But things got tricky when the proponents of algorithmic thinking had to describe what algorithmic thinking was and how it differed from other kinds of thinking. Knuth compared the reasoning patterns in mathematics textbooks and computing textbooks, identifying typical patterns in both.[4] He concluded that algorithmic thinking differed from mathematical thinking in several aspects: by the ways in which it reduces complex problems to interconnected simple ones, emphasizes information structures, pays attention to how actions alter the states of data, and formulates symbolic representations of reality. In his own studies, Dijkstra differentiated computer scientists from mathematicians by their capacity for expressing algorithms in natural as well as formal languages, for devising notations that simplified the computations, for mastering complexity, for shifting between abstraction levels, and for inventing concepts, objects, notations, and theories when necessary.[5]

Today's descriptions of the mental tools of CT are typically much less mathematical in their orientation than were many early descriptions of algorithmic thinking. Over time, many have argued that programming and algorithmic thinking are as important as reading, writing, and arithmetic—the traditional three Rs of education—but the proposal to add them (as a new combined "R") to that list has yet to be accepted. Computing's leaders have a long history of disagreement on this point. Some computing pioneers considered computing's ways of thinking to be a generic tool for everyone, on a par with mathematics and language.[6] Others considered algorithmic thinking to be a rather rare, innate ability—present with about one person in fifty.[7] The former view has more support among educators because it embraces the idea that everyone can learn computational thinking: CT is a skill to be learned and not an ability that one is born with.[8]

The programming and algorithms view of computing spawned new additions to the CT toolbox. The engineering-technology side provided compilers (for converting human-readable programs to executable machine codes), parsing methods (for breaking programming language statements into components), code optimization, operating systems, and empirical testing and debugging methods (for finding errors in programs). The math-science side provided a host of methods for algorithms analysis such as O-notation for estimating the efficiency of algorithms, different models of computation, and proofs of program correctness. By the late 1970s it was clear that computing moved on an intellectual trajectory with concepts, concerns, and skills very different from other academic disciplines.

Computing as Automation

Despite all its richness, the view of computing as the study and design of algorithms was seen as too narrow. By the late 1970s, there were many other questions under investigation. How do you design a new programming language? How do you increase programmer productivity? How do you design a secure operating system? How do you design fault-tolerant software systems and machines? How do you transmit data reliably over a packet network? How do you protect systems against data theft by intruders or malware? How do you find the bottlenecks of a computer system or network? How do you find the response time of a system? How do you get a system to do work previously done by human operators? The study of algorithms focused on individual algorithms but rarely on their interactions with humans or the effects of their computations on other users of systems and networks. It could hardly provide complete answers to these questions.

The idea emerged that the common factor in all these questions, and the soul of computational thinking, was that computing enabled automation in many fields. Automation generally meant one of two things: the control of processes by mechanical means with minimal human intervention, or the carrying out of a process by a machine. Many wanted to return to the 1960s notion that automation was the ultimate purpose of computers and among the most intriguing questions of the modern age. Automation seemed to be the common factor among all of computer science, and CT seemed to be about making automation efficient.

In 1978 the US National Science Foundation launched a comprehensive project to map what is essential in computing. It was called the "Computer Science and Engineering

Research Study" (COSERS). In 1980 they released *What Can Be Automated?*, a thousand-page tome that examined numerous aspects of computing and its applications from the standpoint of efficient automation.[9] That study answered many of the questions above, and for many years, the COSERS report offered the most complete picture of computing and the era's computational thinking. It is still a very relevant resource for anyone who wants an overview, written by famous computing pioneers, of many central themes, problems, and questions in computing.

Well into the 1990s, the computing-as-automation idea was adopted in books, research reports, and influential policy documents as the "fundamental question underlying computing." This idea resonated well with the history of computational thinking: As we discussed in the previous chapters, automatic computing realized the dream of applied mathematicians and engineers to calculate rapidly and correctly without relying on human intuition and judgment. Theoreticians such Alan Turing were fascinated by the idea of mechanizing computing. Practitioners saw their programs as automations of tasks. By 1990, "What can be automated?" became a popular slogan in explanations of computing to outsiders and a carrying theme of computational thinking.

Ironically, the question of "what can be automated" led to the undoing of the automation interpretation because the boundary between what can and cannot be automated is ambiguous. What was previously impossible to automate might now be possible thanks to new algorithms or faster hardware. By the 1970s, computer scientists had developed a rich theory of *computational complexity*, which classified problems according to how many computational steps algorithms solving them needed. For example, searching an unordered list of N items for a specific item takes time proportional to N steps. Sorting a list of N items into ascending order is more complex: it takes time on order of N^2 steps by some algorithms and on order of N $log N$ steps by the best algorithms. Printing a list of all subsets of N items takes time proportional to 2^N. The search problem is of "linear difficulty," the sorting problem is of "quadratic difficulty," and the printing problem is of "exponential difficulty." Search is fast, enumeration is slow; computational complexity theorists call the former "easy" and the latter "hard."

To see how vast the difference is between easy and hard problems, imagine that we have a computer that can do 1 billion (10^9) instructions per second. To search a list of 100 items would take 100 instructions or 0.1 microseconds. To enumerate and print all the subsets of 100 items would take 2^{100} instructions, a process that would take around 10^{14} years. That is 10,000 times longer than the age of the universe, which is very roughly around 10^{10} years old. Even though we can write an algorithm to do that, there is no computer that could complete the job in a reasonable amount of time. Translating this to automation, an algorithm to automate something might take an impossibly long time. Not everything for which we have an algorithm is automatable in practice. Over time, new generations of more powerful machines enable the automation of previously intractable tasks.

Heuristic algorithms make the question of computational hardness even more interesting. The famous knapsack problem asks us to pack a subset of items into a weight-limited knapsack to maximize the value of items packed. The algorithm for doing this is similar to the enumeration problem and would take an impossibly long time for most knapsacks. But we have a rule-of-thumb (a "heuristic") that says "rate each item with its value-weight ratio, and then pack in order of decreasing ratios until the knapsack is full." This rule of thumb packs very good knapsacks fast, but not necessarily the best. Many hard problems are like this. There are fast heuristic algorithms that do a good job but not necessarily the best. We can automate them only if we find a good heuristic algorithm.

The early findings about what things *cannot* be done in computing, either because they are impossible or just too long, led to pessimism about whether computing could help with most practical problems.[10] Today the mood is much more optimistic. A skilled computational thinker uses a sophisticated understanding of computational complexity, logic, and optimization methods to design good heuristic algorithms.

Although all parts of computing contribute to automation, the field of artificial intelligence (AI) has emerged as a focal point in computing for automating human cognitive tasks and other human work. The CT toolbox accumulated heuristic methods for searching solution spaces of games, for deducing conclusions from given information, and for machine-learning methods that find problem solutions by generalizing from examples.

Computing as Pervasive Information Processes

The spread of computing into many fields in the 1990s was another factor in the disintegration of the automation consensus of computational thinking in the academic world. Scientists who ran simulations or evaluated mathematical models were clearly thinking computationally but their interest was not about automating human tasks. A computational interpretation of the universe started to gain a foothold in sciences (see the next section, "The Universe as a Computer"). The nail went into the automation coffin when scientists from other fields started saying around 2000 that they worked with naturally occurring information processes. Biologists, for example, said that the natural process of DNA transcription was computational.

There was nothing to automate; instead they wanted to understand and then modify the process.

Biology is not alone. Cognitive scientists see many brain processes as computational. Chemists see many chemical processes as computational and have designed new materials by computing the reactions that yield them. Drug companies use simulations and search, instead of tedious lab experiments, to find new compounds to treat diseases. Physicists see quantum mechanics as a way to explain all particles and forces as information processes. The list goes on. What is more, many new innovations like blogging, image recognition, encryption, machine learning, natural language processing, and blockchains are all innovations made possible by computing. But none of the above was an automation of any *existing* process—each created an altogether new process.

What a radical change from the days of Newell, Perlis, and Simon! Then the very idea of computer science was attacked because it did not study natural processes. Today much of computing is directly relevant to understanding natural processes.

The Universe as a Computer

Some researchers say there is another stage of evolution beyond this: the idea that the universe is itself a computer.

Computer science's self-story as the field that studies automation faded by the turn of the century. The nail went into the automation coffin when scientists from other fields started saying that they worked with naturally occurring information processes.

Everything we think we see, and everything we think, is computed by a natural process. Instead of using computation to understand nature, they say, we will eventually accept that everything in nature *is* computation. In that case, CT is not just another skill to be learned, it is the natural behavior of the brain.

Hollywood screenwriters love this story line. They have taken it into popular science-fiction movies based on the notion that everything we think we see is produced for us by a computer simulation, and indeed every thought we think we have is an illusion given by a computation. It might be an engaging story, but there is little evidence to support it.

This claim is a generalization of a distinction familiar in artificial intelligence. *Strong AI* refers to the belief that suitably programmed machines can *be* literally intelligent. *Weak AI* refers to the belief that, through smart programming, machines can simulate mental activities so well they *appear* intelligent without being intelligent. For example, virtual assistants like Siri and Alexa are weak AI because they do a good job at recognizing common commands and acting on them without "understanding" them.

The pursuit for strong AI dominated the AI agenda from the founding of the AI field in 1950 until the late 1990s. It produced very little insight into intelligence and no machines came close to anything that could be considered intelligent in the same way humans are intelligent.

The pursuit for specialized, weak AI applications rose to ascendance beginning in the 1990s and is responsible for the amazing innovations with neural networks and big data analysis.

Similar to the weak-strong distinction in AI, the "strong" computational view of the universe holds that the universe itself, along with every living being, is a digital computer. Every dimension of space and time is discrete and every movement of matter or energy is a computation. In contrast, the "weak" computational view of the universe does not claim that the world computes, but only that computational interpretations of the world are very useful for studying phenomena: we can model, simulate, and study the world using computation.

The strong computational view is highly speculative, and while it has some passionate proponents, it faces numerous problems both empirical and philosophical. Its rise is understandable as a continuation of the ongoing quest to understand the world through the latest available technology. For instance, in the Age of Enlightenment, the world was compared to the clockwork. The brain has successively been compared to the mill, the telegraph system, hydraulic systems, electromagnetic systems, and the computer. The newest stage in this progression is to interpret the world is not a classical computer but a quantum computer.

SOFTWARE ENGINEERING

Software engineering is the part of computer science
that is too difficult for the computer scientist.
—Fritz Bauer (1971)

At 9:10 p.m. on July 22, 1962, access arms retracted
from the 33-meter-tall Mariner I rocket that stood on
the launch pad in Cape Canaveral. On top sat a hexago-
nal magnesium frame packed with high-tech electronics
for gathering, analyzing, computing, and communicating
scientific data, and an operating system to keep all the
systems alive. Destined for Venus, Mariner I was the first
of a series of 10 interplanetary NASA probes to do flyby
surveys of Mars, Mercury, and Venus. It was the first
flyby of another planet in history. Years of work by thousands of people planning, calculating, designing, testing, and building the vessel culminated at that moment.

Mariner I was also aiming to get the US ahead of the Soviet Union in the space race. Ten minutes and dozens of checks later the flight control gave a go for final countdown.

Seconds after the rocket fired off toward a new world, monitoring equipment started to indicate problems. The rocket's system for tracking and sending velocity data did not work correctly. The ground control computers were supposed to take over—usually no big deal, as that is what backup systems are for. But somewhere in the long time it took to develop the computer system, someone had missed a tiny punctuation detail in the program, which led the computer to base its decisions on raw data instead of data smoothed over a time window. That error led the rocket to overcompensate for minor perturbations in its trajectory, steering it uncontrollably toward inhabited areas and shipping lanes. At 293 seconds after the liftoff, ground control had no choice but to send a destruct command to the vehicle. Tons of metal, high-tech electronics, and rocket fuel rained down into the Atlantic Ocean.

Initial reports of what caused the massively publicized failure were out within a week, mostly citing that small mistake in the computer program. The *New York Times* headline was, "For Want of Hyphen Venus Rocket Is Lost." That sobering moment pushed the concept of programming error into the public consciousness. Many people's eyes opened to the potentially disastrous consequences of software failure. By the end of the 1960s, reports of software problems were commonplace. Software errors impaired reliability, undercut productivity, and sometimes posed serious dangers.

Software developers realized that the era's computational thinking was not capable of delivering reliable and dependable software. Most CT was about thinking in the small—practices and thinking tools for single programmers. There was nothing in CT for thinking in the large—practices and thinking tools for teams of programmers developing large-scale production systems with long life spans and large user bases. Here in this chapter we investigate the important shift of scale in computational thinking and the difficulties it caused.

Software Crises

The early years of the stored-program computer were a triumph of computer engineering. Hardware development, from the "computing super-brain" to the "awesome thinking machine," made the headlines. The press featured room-sized reckoning behemoths weighing tens of tons that operated a thousand times faster than the previous computing machinery and, most importantly, could calculate thousands of times faster than the world's best mathematicians. Mathematics and logic were celebrated as the feature that distinguished humans from beasts—and now machines could do both.

The early enthusiasm for computers soon moved beyond "makin' numbers"—as one computing pioneer called scientific computing—to processing data in symbols that can stand for any information at all. Magazines and newspapers gave examples of computers doing tasks that were previously seen as the sole province of humans: one group programmed the computer to play checkers, another chess, another to automatically prove theorems in the monumental *Principia Mathematica*, and another built a mechanical mouse that searched its way through a maze. The uses of computers in business, science, and engineering applications multiplied each year. All these advances came from software. The computer revolution began with hardware, but soon became a revolution of software.

The size and complexity of computer programs grew rapidly. Dark clouds began to hover over software development. Developers were becoming painfully aware of great difficulties in their ability to make production-quality software—software that was dependable, reliable, usable, safe, and secure. The intellectual and management tools developed up to that time were not powerful enough to build such software. Developers began to speak of a "software crisis."

In two famous meetings sponsored by NATO in 1968 and 1969, software developers turned to engineering for a solution to the frequent and sometimes catastrophic failures of software. The movement was labeled "software engineering." Engineering had long traditions for consistently producing reliable systems. It was rare for bridges to fall, planes to crash, or infrastructure to fail massively. Software engineers rapidly began to import and develop engineering ways into software development and software product management.

An early focus in software engineering was the design of "abstractions," which are simplified models of something complicated with a simple interface. Good abstractions hide the details of the machinery implementing them, allowing programmers to debug them without having to dig into the details of underlying machines. For example, a file is presented as a container of a string of bits with two operations, read and write; its complicated implementation as records scattered across a hard disk is completely hidden. Designing hierarchies of abstractions is seen as the only way to master the enormous complexity of software. Finding good abstractions is an essential design skill for programmers and software engineers. Programming languages that allow programmers to express their abstractions are essential.[1]

In his classic book *The Mythical Man-Month* (1975), the software pioneer Fred Brooks noted two dimensions for transforming programs into production systems. One was the generalization of a single software program to a system of interacting programs. The other was the addition of structures and components that provided guarantees to make the software reliable. His rule of thumb was that movement in either dimension tripled the effort. Movement in both dimensions was needed to achieve reliable production systems—a total of nine times the effort of creating a single program.

Software developers, having become aware of such a wide gap between basic programming and production systems, had to find new practices of CT to close it. They developed a trove of new forms of CT: new practices for decomposition, complexity, information structures, causality, closing semantic gaps, data abstraction, data structures, encapsulation, information hiding, recursion, project management, and software life cycles. Aspects of theoretical computer science, notably complexity theory and automatic theorem proving, became helpful in this arena.

The movement described by Brooks can be characterized as moving from computational thinking *in the small* (designing and writing single programs) to computational thinking *in the large* (designing software systems and managing the software projects that build them from design and into production and maintenance).

Science and Engineering in Computing

A scientific revolution began in the mid-1500s. For much of the time since, there was little practical difference between science and engineering; scientists look for principles of phenomena and engineers built technologies that exploited the phenomena. Many scientists were engineers and many engineers were scientists. The sharp distinction we see today between science and engineering is recent.[2] The distinction was introduced in the late 1940s when Vannevar Bush advocated the establishment of the US National Science Foundation for government support of basic research. Since that time, academic programs have come to define engineering as the "application of science and mathematics to solve problems of use to people"—in effect defining engineering as a subset of science. This definition hides the unique contributions engineering can make to software. It obscures the need for interaction between the science and engineering sides of computing to make software reliable.

We have found three distinctions between engineering and science particularly helpful to understand the contributions each can make to software production. The first concerns the nature of their work. Engineers design and build technologies that serve useful purposes, whereas scientists search for laws explaining and predicting phenomena. *Design* is among the most commonly used words of engineering, whereas it is uncommon in science. Design in engineering is a process of finding practical, safe, cost-effective implementations. Scientists concentrate on finding and validating recurrences, engineers on listening to clients and proposing technologies of value to them.

The second main distinction is how scientists and engineers regard knowledge. Scientists treat knowledge as data and information that have been organized into a "body of knowledge," which is then available for anyone to use. The scientific method for creating knowledge is a process of standard, disinterested observers gathering and weighing evidence in support of claims that might be added to the body. Engineers treat knowledge as skillful practices that enable design and building of tools and technologies. Engineers are not outside observers; they are immersed in the communities of use. They embody practices for building, maintaining, and repairing technologies; attending to reliability, dependability, and safety in the context of use; and following engineering standards and codes of ethics.

The third main distinction concerns the role of abstractions and models. Science emphasizes models, and engineering emphasizes machines and artifacts. There is a fundamental distinction between modeling machines and building them. Abstractions are useful for what they leave out. Machines are useful for what they leave in. Hardware and software are interchangeable to the theorist, but not to the engineer.

The familiar phrase "the devil is in the details" is an engineer's motto. Engineers must get the details right for systems to work. Scientists want to eliminate the details so that the recurrences stand out.

These differences explain why it has been hard to design software engineering education that actually produces capable software developers. Many software engineering groups are in computer science departments that emphasize the science over engineering. The same balancing problem haunts computational thinking, too: when one or the other worldview dominates, the synergies are lost.

Computational Thinking in the Small

A computing pioneer who worked with one of the first computers wrote in his memoir that he still remembered the day when he suddenly realized he would be spending most of the rest of his life looking for mistakes in his own programs.[3] In the 1950s, everyone came to believe this—it was very hard to write programs that worked correctly. Programming was unexplored territory to everyone. Initially, all the first programmers could do was borrow ideas and techniques from other fields and use their ingenuity to get programs to work. Nothing seemed to help avoid making errors while programming. What was earlier envisaged to be a straightforward translation of high-level algorithmic plans to machine instructions was found to be a complex of challenges from incomplete problem specifications, machine idiosyncrasies, poor performance, memory limitations, and debugging. Getting computers work turned out to be an endless cycle of accommodations to surprises and obstacles.

As a result, programming in the 1950s developed an aura of mystique. Programming language pioneers remembered that aura vividly in their memoirs. One wrote that programming in the 1950s was "a black art, a private arcane matter involving only a programmer, a problem, a computer, and perhaps a small library of subroutines. ... Programmers started to regard themselves as members of a priesthood guarding skills and mysteries far too complex for ordinary mortals." Another described later how the programmers of the 1950s loved their obscure codes and tricks.[4] Yet another wrote that it took until the 1960s before programming started to evolve from a craft to a science. He marveled at how, despite their "primitive" way of thinking about programming, programmers of the 1950s were able to create so many useful programs.[5] Computational thinking of the early computer era was rich but fragmented, and focused on making single programs work on specific machinery.

Many pioneers of computing worked to make the programmer's job easier and less error-prone. They did this by developing and refining programming methodology and programming languages, and by designing sophisticated operating systems. Their innovations began with structural principles for modularity in the machines of the 1950s, which led to computational thinkers starting to increasingly think in terms of subroutines, macros that abbreviated often-used pieces of code, separately compiled modules, linkers that combine compiled modules into full programs, libraries of ready-to-run executable modules, and version control systems that tracked all the software modules built and modified by a team. All these tools helped manage program complexity and reduce errors.

As they gained familiarity with the practices of programming, language designers developed higher-level languages, such as FORTRAN and COBOL around 1958. These languages enabled programmers to express algorithmic statements that were automatically translated by compiler into machine code; they relieved programmers of the burden of direct machine code programming. When they saw that programmers often started by designing the data structures and then a small set of subroutines that performed operations on the structures, language designers enunciated the practice of *data abstraction*. Data abstraction matured into object-oriented programming languages. Data abstraction has become another key feature of CT: it hides internal mechanisms of program components, while allowing the use of those components through well-defined interfaces. With data abstraction, programmers can focus more easily on *what* the components do rather than *how* they do it.

Operating systems designers contributed a raft of important precepts to CT during that same era. Operating systems allow many users to share a single machine by scheduling resources, resolving conflicts, allocating memory among user programs, and multiplexing computing jobs on the processors. Operating systems designers introduced the idea of a system being a "society of cooperating processes," where a process is an independently executing program in private memory that cannot be accessed by other processes, and where each process stands by to perform a specific service when requested. Operating systems designers invented virtual memory to automate data transfers between memory levels, file systems to store and protect user data, and interprocess messaging systems to exchange data and requests. They invented kernels to provide a professionally built and highly trusted set of programs for all basic operating system functions. Kernels isolated processes and prevented errors in any one from affecting any other.

Today's CT inherits many precepts for programming methodology including modularity, abstraction, information hiding, hierarchical composition, recursion, design patterns, managing digital objects, visualization, verification, and debugging. These conceptual tools require great skill and experience at design. Design has emerged as one of the major areas of development in computing; we will discuss it in depth in chapter 6. CT precepts on languages, methodology, and operating systems all aid productivity and confine or eliminate errors.

Many of those practices became so ingrained in CT that for decades computational problem-solvers have considered them to be basic building blocks of CT. These engineering developments complemented the mathematical side of programming, which in those days focused on structuring programs to facilitate formal proof of their correctness and practices such as the use of recursion.

Software Development Drifts into a Crisis

With all these advances in CT, why did a software crisis develop? In the 1950s computing, the machine was the product. Software—as the control programs for the machines—was not something to be packaged and sold. Most programmers focused on programs for their personal or immediate workgroup use, but not on programs to use outside their organization. The computational thinking tools for "programming in the small" supported personal use well, but not large-scale development of complex software products.

A software industry began to evolve from a few software contractors in the 1950s to corporate software developers in the 1960s, and then to mass-market software in the 1970s and beyond. In each of these decades, the revenues of the software industry grew tenfold.

In the 1960s software developers found that selling software was no gravy train. More and more software projects ended up late, over budget, bug-ridden to a point of being useless, or never delivered at all. Post-delivery software maintenance, improvement, and bug fixing were costly, difficult, and sometimes infeasible. Software systems frequently contained lurking bugs that made their applications unsafe for humans or caused expensive failures such as the loss of the Mariner spacecraft.

Software developers who had little familiarity with the target domain often caused large gaps between customer needs and the functions of computational systems. Software developers found that the known principles of design were not up to the task of providing dependable, reliable, usable, safe, and secure software—known as the DRUSS objectives. Professional programmers realized that their computational-thinking skills did not scale up well: something was qualitatively different about a program written by a single programmer and a system that required a team of 300 programmers.

Software companies tried to minimize these problems in two ways. One was to hire highly skilled programmers who could produce many times more code per day with significantly fewer errors than entry-level programmers. Salaries for good programmers shot up: software developers became one of the highest-paid professions in the US.

The other way was to abdicate liability for errors. Software companies adopted a "non-warranty"—licensing the software to a user only after the user agreed that the company would not be liable for damages caused by errors in the code. This policy contributed strongly to public disillusionment with the computer revolution.

Leading software developers admitted that their tools for programming in the small were simply not up to programming in the large. They had passed the limits of reliable software construction. A number of leading software industry figures, academics, and software developers declared a software crisis and organized the 1968–1969 NATO conferences to address it.

Computational Thinking in the Large

What happens when we go from single programs with single users to systems of many programs with many users? The skills and competences required to write a program of a thousand lines of code are different from those to build software of a million lines of code. The main reason is that large software systems have to be built by teams. Software developers had to learn how to organize and manage teams for successful software development.

Fred Brooks was the manager of a team of 300 programmers who built the IBM 360 operating system in the 1960s. Their system eventually grew to a massive 10 million lines of code. In his book, *The Mythical Man-Month* (1975), Brooks documented his experience in detail and gave rules of thumb of CT for organizing and designing large systems. One of his famous observations is that time and people do not trade off equally: a team of 12 programmers cannot complete in a month a job that took a single programmer 12 months. Another is that the structure of the software winds up resembling the organization that built it. Brooks concluded that managing the team was a greater challenge than the technology problems the team had to solve.

Although the attendees at the NATO conferences agreed that there was a major "software problem" and that engineering principles might help, they had little agreement on what kind of engineering would do the job. The traditional engineers looked to fault tolerant design, systems thinking, and project management. Theoretically oriented computer scientists looked to mathematical proof (formal verification) to establish that software met its specifications without error and introduced methods such as structured programming and algorithms analysis to facilitate understanding and proofs of programs.

Neither approach made much of a dent in the software problem. Traditional systems engineering did not work well because of a crucial difference between software and large physical systems, such as bridges, buildings, planes, and ships: an error in a single bit of code can cause catastrophic failure such as the crash of a rocket whereas the loss of a minute sliver of material might degrade a large system but would not crash it. Mathematical proof did not work well because it was too difficult for large systems, it said nothing about human aspects such as usability, and it did not address problems in the hardware such as component failures or noise corrupting signals. The software pioneers Brian Randell and Fred Brooks were among the most prescient in saying why software systems are so much harder. Randell said the problem was not programming per se but "multi-person development of multi-version programs." Brooks, in his 1975 book, said that productizing a program by turning it into a system that could be used safely and reliably by non-programmers was far more challenging than writing the program in the first place.

Design Principles, Patterns, and Hints

Skillful design can make enormous improvements in the size and complexity of software. Operating systems are a good example. Modern operating systems such as Windows 10, MacOS X, or Linux approach 100 million lines of code. It is a triumph of software engineering to produce such systems with very good reliability. All these systems contain a "kernel," the set of software functions for very basic operations in the system such as starting execution of a program, exchanging messages between programs, or reading files. The functions of kernels have changed little since the 1970s but kernel sizes have exploded from around 20 thousand instructions in early systems to 20 million today—a factor of 1000. The increased size has increased vulnerability to attacks. Nicklaus Wirth attributes this to waste of cheap resources—processor cycles and storage bits. He wrote:

> This waste has become ever-present and represents a grave lack of sense for quality. Inefficiency of programs is easily covered up by obtaining faster processors, and poor data design by the use of larger storage devices. But their side effect is a decrease of quality—of reliability, robustness, and ease of use. Good, careful design is time consuming, costly. But it is still cheaper than unreliable, difficult software,

when the cost of "maintenance" is factored in. The trend is disquieting, and so is the complacency of customers. (Wirth 2008)

The goals of programming in the large were summarized as the five DRUSS objectives – dependable, reliable, usable, safe, and secure. To achieve these goals software developers work with three kinds of computational thinking practices: design principles, patterns, and hints.

Design principles are descriptions of skills and strategies that developers follow when making design decisions. The principles guide them toward designs that meet the five DRUSS objectives.

Design patterns are descriptions of common situations a programmer is likely to encounter. They offer guidance on how to structure the program, or on the process of writing it, for best results.

Design hints are rules of thumb or morsels of advice, most useful to those with advanced skills at systems development.

Principles

The classic paper by Jerome Saltzer and Michael Schroeder about information protection is an excellent example of design principles (see table 5.1).[6] Design principles are ways of thinking about the total system of software components, in order to achieve the DRUSS objectives and

Table 5.1 Information Protection Principles of Saltzer and Schroeder

Principle	Directive
Economy of mechanism	Keep the design simple and small.
Fail-safe defaults	Deny access by default; grant access only by explicit permission.
Complete mediation	Check every access to every object.
Open design	Do not depend on attackers being ignorant of the design.
Separation of privilege	Grant access based on more than one piece of information.
Least privilege	Force every process to operate with the minimum privileges needed for its task.
Least common mechanism	Make shared state information inaccessible to individual processes, lest one corrupt it.
Psychological acceptability	Protection should be easy to use, at least as easy as not using it.

reduce compromise of sensitive information. The principles are embodied in the skills and ways of thinking that system developers acquire over time from building complex computing systems. They apply to any large system that accommodates many users and service processes.

Patterns

In the early 1990s a group of programmers founded the "software pattern community" movement, inspired by the design-pattern idea of building architect Christopher Alexander.[7] Their idea was that if they could describe a common pattern of software use that has been solved by skilled programmers, they could distill the pattern's essence so that other programmers can imitate it. A software pattern characterizes a large number of situations a programmer is likely to encounter and offers guidance on how to structure the program to best fit the pattern.[8] The number of recognized patterns runs in dozens. Examples are the singleton pattern, which limits the number of instances of an object to one, and the iterator pattern, which implements sequential access to data elements. The pattern community appeals to a sense of empiricism because its members are relentless about testing ideas with potential users and learning from the feedback.

Hints

Butler Lampson, a superb and accomplished designer, summarized a number of guidelines for advanced designers of operating systems.[9] He said: "Designing a computer system is very different from designing an algorithm. The external interface is less precisely defined, more complex, and more subject to change. The system has much more internal structure and hence many internal interfaces. And the measure of success is unclear." He said the less skilled designers often flounder in seas of possibilities, not knowing how a current choice will affect future choices of the performance of the system. He called his statements "design hints" because they are judgments skilled designers learn to make over time; they emphasize the considerable art in designing. In table 5.2 we list Lampson's hints for three dimensions of system development (rows) and major aspects of the DRUSS objectives (columns). Though they may appear as generalities, they are quite meaningful in shaping the CT skills of advanced designers.

Table 5.2 Lampson's Design Hints

	Correctness & Fit	Speed	Fault Tolerance
Use cases	Separate normal and worst cases	Safety first Shed load End-to-end	End-to-end
Interface	Keep it simple Do one thing well Don't generalize Get it right Don't hide power Use procedure arguments Leave it to the client Keep interface stable Keep a place to stand	Make it fast Split resources Static analysis Dynamic translation	End-to-end Log updates Make actions atomic
Implementation	Plan to throw one away Keep secrets Reuse a good idea Divide and conquer	Cache answers Use hints Use brute force Compute in background Batch processing	Make actions atomic Use hints

Design Principles for Software

The software engineering literature records a large number of design principles that have been widely studied and found to be strongly supportive of good design. The very best of these principles have been encoded as structures that appear in languages, application programs, and operating systems. They are mentioned frequently in discussions of CT and their roots lie in many different intellectual traditions described in earlier chapters of this book. They are in three main categories:

Hierarchical aggregation

Virtual machines

Clients-servers

These structures are intended as tools to help with recurrent patterns that designers encounter.

Hierarchical Aggregation

Hierarchical aggregation means that objects (identifiable software and hardware components) consist of groups of smaller objects connected by well-defined interfaces. You can interact with an object as a unity through its interface and not be concerned with its individual parts. When you do look inside, you need not be concerned with what is going on in the external environment. Thus, there is a hierarchy with smaller aggregates making up larger aggregates. Aggregates at every level of the hierarchy are insulated from lower- and higher-level details.

There is a long list of aspects of hierarchical modularity. *Decomposition* means to subdivide a large system into smaller, manageable components. *Modularity* is a process of implementing the components as modules that can be designed separately, compiled separately, stored separately, and then assembled into the full system. The modules interact across precisely defined *interfaces*. Modules can be stored in libraries and *reused* for other purposes. *Abstraction* means to define a simplified version of something and to state the operations (functions) that apply to it. *Levels* are a structural form in which peer components share a common interface.[10] *Information hiding* conceals the details of an implementation from users, protecting users against errors caused by changes in the details and protecting the module from errors caused by external changes. *Encapsulation* goes further, by shielding anything outside an untrusted module from errors within the module.

The *object* concept is an advanced form of encapsulation; it originated with a programming practice called "data abstraction" in the 1960s and evolved into over a hundred sophisticated object-oriented languages today. An object is an abstract entity that can be viewed and altered only through a defined set of operations. Its internal structure and state are hidden. For example, a file appears to users as a container of a sequence of bits and can be acted on only with the open, close, read, or write operations; its hidden internal structure is a set of records scattered across a disk. The disk structure of a file is irrelevant to users and hence hidden from them. A *class* of objects is a set of objects with the same interface; the classes are organized into a hierarchy of their own. Novice programmers often find objects confusing because they do not yet understand abstract machines, information hiding, and synchronization.

Virtual Machines

A virtual machine is a simulation of one computer by another. Alan Turing's universal machine was the first example. Today the term *virtual machine* is used in a number of ways. First, it means the simulation of any abstract computing machine; it is the platform on which computations can run.

Second, virtual machines are simulations of hardware computers. The virtual machine has subroutines that carry out the effect of the machine instructions on the hardware computer. This idea came into practice in the late 1950s when a second generation of computers began to replace the first generation. The new computers had to run all the software written for previous versions of the computer. Accordingly, manufacturers provided an "emulation mode" in which the new computer could simulate the instructions of the older computer it replaced. The emulation mode has matured in the form of VMware and Hyper-V, which simulate entire computers running their own operating systems. The ubiquitous Java Virtual Machines (JVM) emulate Java on any commercial machine by executing the Java "byte code" produced by Java compilers, allowing great portability of Java programs.

Third, virtual machines are simulations of a host machine within separate memory partitions of the host machine. This is the organizing principle of the IBM VM 370 and later operating systems. The IBM virtual machine is a complete simulation of an IBM mainframe, identical in every way to the original except that it has a reduced main memory. This approach allows the virtual machine to run at nearly the same speed as the real machine; there is no significant performance loss.

Fourth, a virtual machine is a standard environment for implementing any program within an operating system. This idea was pioneered in the Multics system at MIT (1968) and the UNIX system at Bell Labs (1972). These operating systems featured many "processes," each a program in execution on a virtual machine. The virtual machine was simply a standard template for providing input and output to a running program and connecting with any submachines it may have spawned. Every user program would be embedded into the standard virtual machine for execution.

Clients and Servers

The client server model is a conceptually simple way to organize interactions between processes in a distributed (networked) computing system. A server is a process dedicated to performing a particular service on request. A client is another process that makes requests. Clients and servers are usually (but not always) on different hosts in a network. Their requests and responses are passed as messages through the network. For example, a network file server stores all the files of the network's users; client processes on user workstations send it requests to read and write files. An authentication server interacts with the login client on a user's workstation to process the user's credentials during login. A web server interacts with client browsers to send them web pages.

Although the client server idea is simple, its implementations are often far from simple. Designers must master many subtle details to get communications, error control, and synchronization working correctly.

No Silver Bullet

In 1987, Frederick Brooks wrote "No Silver Bullet," a famous assessment of progress in software engineering since 1968. His conclusions held important lessons for CT. He said that two main complexity factors affect our ability to produce reliable software. The limitations of the technology are the first factor, but they can be overcome by improved technologies, such as high-level programming languages, interactive program development environments, visualization of control and data flow, faster hardware, and better operating systems.

The second factor is our own mental ability to comprehend the essence of complex problems. Coping with complexity is intrinsic to software design and construction and will never go away. The design problem, Brooks said, is mostly conceptual—getting an intellectual grasp on the functions of the system to provide and organize a simple and elegant design.

To address it, we need to grow large systems in relatively easy increments, reuse existing software as much as possible, and make more use of rapid prototyping to gain early feedback before technical decisions are locked. Most of all, Brooks said, we need to "cultivate great designers." He saw coping with complexity as an essential skill requiring great mastery. Brooks famously wrote that there is "no silver bullet" that will kill the werewolf of complexity in software development.

The "software problem" articulated in the NATO conferences was mostly concerned with programmer productivity and the chronic problem of errors causing unreliable

The main factor imped-
ing reliable software
is our own mental
ability to comprehend
the essence of complex
problems. Coping with
complexity is intrinsic
to software design
and construction and
will never go away.

programs. Since those days new developments have added to the complexities of software design. These include:

Malware and intruders: Criminals and hackers intentionally hunt for bugs in complex programs and exploit them for theft of data, destruction of data, and even ransoms to unlock purposely encrypted data.

Fault tolerance: Even if the software has been proved to be correct, the proof depends on assumptions that the underlying hardware always works as intended. Hardware itself is now so complex that proving it correct is a major challenge of its own. Many hardware bugs have been detected in supposedly well-tested chips. Not only that, but hardware can wear out and start malfunctioning because of component failures or because unexpected events in the world throw it into unstable states. Hardware engineers have increasingly been concerned with fault tolerance, that is, designs that tolerate such faults—for example, a system that shuts itself down rather than perform a critical operation incorrectly. This kind of hardware fault tolerance, which involves extra circuits that monitor each other, cannot be done with any software structure. Software correctness proofs are not sufficient for correct operation.

Secure hardware: Most attacks on computer systems occur at the lowest levels of the kernel and network where efficient dynamic monitoring is most difficult to do. In the 1960s there was considerable interest in hardware design that would facilitate information protection by limiting the spread of errors and blocking software attempts to circumvent permissions. Highly advanced architectures were designed that enabled encapsulation of untrusted programs and severely limited error propagation.

Unfortunately, these advances were lost in the "RISC revolution" of the 1980s. To build faster CPUs, computer designers eliminated hundreds of instructions from CPUs, reducing them to highly simplified, very fast chips. They called the new generation of chips Reduced Instruction Set Computers (RISC). The reductions eliminated the hardware extensions for encapsulating and monitoring software.

Today, security experts want to reinstate the extra hardware monitoring to block the low-level attacks by malware and intruders. Secure hardware is making a comeback. A complicating factor is the fact that many companies outsource production of their chips, making it possible for third parties to insert backdoors into the hardware that allow intruders easy access to the system.

Machine learning algorithms: The recent explosion of artificial intelligence (AI) is due primarily to rapid growth in neural network technologies. When the training process of a neural network is done, no one knows why the internal connection weights are what they are or how to prove the network is correct for untrained inputs. Similarly, there are no hardware monitors to detect when a neural network is about to go bad. This has been called the fragility problem: To what extent can we trust the AI to do the right thing when presented with inputs outside its training data?

Safety: Many software systems are used in safety critical applications, where an error in the software can cause catastrophic loss of life or property.

Mass production of diverse software applications: Today's mobile apps, games, desktop widgets, and network-based systems have little in common with the software of the 1960s and 1970s. There was little outsourcing of software development to trusted third parties. There were no large networks of application developers selling through app stores before the early 2000s; the Apple and Android stores now offer millions of apps.

Computational thinking is being constantly challenged to grow and deal with these contemporary problems.

DESIGNING FOR HUMANS

Descriptions of software entities that abstract away
their complexity often abstract away their essence. Good
judgment comes from experience, and experience comes
from bad judgment.

—Frederick Brooks (1986)

We are searching for some kind of harmony between two
intangibles: a form which we have not yet designed and
a context which we cannot properly describe. Making
simulations of what you're going to build is tremendously
useful if you can get feedback from them that will tell you
where you've gone wrong and what you can do about it.

— Christopher Alexander (1964)

Among computing's early pioneers, George Forsythe was
one of the first to advocate that computing deals primarily

with issues related to design: design of computers and systems, design of languages for processors and algorithms, and design of methods for representing and processing information.[1] Software engineers were among the first within computing to explicitly treat design as an essential part of the discipline's practice. For software engineers, design meant planning and construction of software products and systems that met their specifications and were safe and reliable. Design also meant creating tools to support software construction including related languages, editors, voice command and graphical interfaces, project management practices, version control systems, and development environments.[2] The recent proliferation of useful applications through commercial "app stores" has brought a lot of people who are not formally trained in software engineering into software design.

But there is more to design than building systems. Design is familiar in many fields including fashion, products, and architecture. It is a process of creating and shaping artifacts that address human concerns. In software, for example, design means crafting software that does jobs users want done. Software designers do far more than build to meet functional specifications. They intentionally support practices, worlds, contexts, and identities of the software's users. The famous success of the iPhone is attributed not only to its considerable technical prowess, but also to the identities and fashion statements iPhone users project. There have also been notorious failures attributed to poor design that promoted unsafe use of systems, such as aircraft panel displays that did not show the most needed information in emergencies.[3]

We discussed in chapter 5 how software engineers have accumulated much practical wisdom that is expressed with design principles, patterns, and hints, all in pursuit of the DRUSS (dependable, reliable, usable, safe, and secure) objectives. But design concerns go much further than just improving the software construction process.

Despite the successes of software engineering, software project failures and accidents continue to accumulate. Academics continue to struggle with software engineering curricula that can graduate professional software developers who can lead projects to completion without failure. David Parnas, a famous software pioneer, says that this academic quest is doomed in many departments because most curriculum attempts have tried to identify and teach a "software engineering body of knowledge" rather than the capabilities of proficient professional software designers.[4] Computing students are taught structural rules for software but not the design skills required to achieve good software. Table 6.1 summarizes the capabilities Parnas believes are the most important. All these capabilities are oriented toward the user communities and are not restricted to formal aspects of software development process. Design CT guides us to ways of building computing

Design is familiar in many fields including fashion, products, and architecture. It is a process of creating and shaping artifacts that address human concerns. In software, design means crafting software that does jobs users want done.

Table 6.1   Capabilities of Software Developers

- Design human-computer interfaces
- Design and maintain multi-version, reusable software
- Ensure that software products meet quality and security standards
- Create and use models in system development
- Specify, predict, analyze, and evaluate performance
- Be disciplined in development and maintenance
- Use metrics in system development
- Manage complex projects

systems whose behaviors are useful and meaningful in their user communities.

What Is Design?

Many software developers have turned to design for new thinking that would lead away from the software morass. The long history of design in computing has left many questions open for the designers: What is the difference between software engineering and design? Why has it taken 50 years for the early declarations on design to become a prominent concern? How important is design to CT?

The software engineering approach to design is a semiformal methodology to craft a set of modules and interfaces to achieve a stated functional purpose. The purpose is captured in a set of requirements, each a specific, testable statement. A traditional engineering process moves from requirements to a working, delivered system:

Requirements

Formal specifications

System construction

Acceptance testing

Delivery to the customer

Software engineers can carry out this process in private, bypassing any interaction with the users in between the requirement and delivery stages. The process is attuned to the early notions in computing that software is machine-executable code for algorithms that meet given functional specifications, and that programmers need quiet time to get things right.

But experience has shown that the traditional engineering process is prone to break down with complex systems. Roughly a third of software projects deliver on time and within budget, another third deliver late or over budget, and the remainder never deliver. One of the biggest challenges is the sheer number of modules and interfaces that must be designed, programmed, tracked, and tested—modern operating systems, for example, consist of hundreds of thousands of modules. Another big

The software engineering approach to design is a semi-formal methodology to craft a set of modules and interfaces to achieve a stated functional purpose. The design approach focuses on the virtual world created by the software, the practices that engage users in that world, and the user concerns addressed by that world.

challenge is getting the requirements right: many software projects meet their formal requirements only to be judged deficient by their customers. From the engineer's standpoint, a necessary requirement was left out. From the user's standpoint, the missing requirement was obvious to any member of the community. The disconnect is that something obvious to the community may not be obvious to the engineer, who was not aware of an issue that was part of unstated user context.

Engineers responded to these breakdowns by trying to improve the construction process. They developed sophisticated interview methods to elicit requirements from customers and thus minimize the risk that an important requirement was left out. They codified "design patterns" followed by successful designers, so that less experienced designers could avoid mistakes. They introduced "agile methods" for project management that explicitly involved customers through all stages of the engineering project. Agile product management often features many, rapidly iterated prototypes under constant review by teams that include customer representatives.

These process improvements slowed but did not stem the tide of system failures. Some designers advocated a radical shift of thinking. Terry Winograd, a pioneer in artificial intelligence and design, characterized the shift in this way:[5]

The education of computer professionals has often concentrated on the understanding of computational mechanisms, and on engineering methods that are intended to ensure that the mechanisms behave as the programmer intends. The focus is on the objects being designed: the hardware and software. The primary concern is to implement a specified functionality efficiently. When software engineers or programmers say that a piece of software works, they typically mean that it is robust, is reliable, and meets its functional specification. These concerns are indeed important. Any designer who ignores them does so at the risk of disaster.

But this inward-looking perspective, with its focus on function and construction, is one-sided. To design software that really works, we need to move from a constructor's-eye view to a designer's-eye view, taking the system, the users, and the context all together as a starting point. When a designer says that something works (for example, a layout for a book cover or a design for a housing complex), the term reflects a broader meaning. Good design produces an object that works for people in a context of values and needs, to produce quality results and a satisfying experience.

Winograd and others introduced the term *virtual world* for the focus of software design. Software creates a world—a context in which a user of the software perceives, acts, and responds to experiences. A user who enters the world and behaves according to its rules and logic is called an *inhabitant* because the world seems real during the time the user is in it. The key point is that the virtual world is not a mental construct of user or designer, it is an experience that seems real.

Online games are examples of virtual worlds. In them the players defeat monsters, seek out treasures, earn achievements for quests, and advance in level and experience. Many players say that the world of the game is as real as the everyday world when they are in it. These games create a world by having a definite purpose, a playing field and equipment, norms and values, rules for allowable and unallowable behavior, and strategies for winning or advancing. But the idea of creating a world is not limited to entertainment games. Today's social networks, and services such as Uber, Airbnb, and eBay, all look like multi-player games, where the possibilities available to you as a player evolve and shift according to the choices and actions of others. Even single-user software such as spreadsheets, word processors, and drawing programs all create worlds of their own in which there is a well-defined playing field and a set of basic rules and strategies for all to follow.

Since 2005, when Apple introduced the App Store and made iPhones infinitely customizable as users downloaded apps (applications) that suited them, there has been an explosion of software development of apps. The Apple and Android online app stores combined offer more than 6 million apps. Software has become a market commodity. Only the apps judged by their many customers as "high quality" make it in this market.

Software Quality and Satisfaction

In the 1970s, software engineers sought to make software quality measurable, on the time-honored premise that we get more of what we measure. They devised models for measuring software quality. Their models eventually became a standard of the ISO (International Standards Organization), and a central building block of computational thinking in software engineering. The ISO standards list 20 measurable factors to assess overall quality of a software system:

correctness

reliability

integrity

usability

efficiency

maintainability

testability

interoperability

flexibility

reusability

portability

clarity

modifiability

documentation

resilience

understandability

validity

functionality

generality

economy

These measures were all intended to be objectively measurable properties of the software. It is very hard to design a software system that scores high on all 20 factors.

Two of the five traditional DRUSS objectives—security and safety—are not on this list because no one knew how to measure software for these aspects. No one said that quality is simple and straightforward.

The new and burgeoning market for apps has brought attention to quality as an assessment of users rather than as a property of the software. Quality is in the eye of the beholder. Much more attention is paid to design in the sense that Winograd has defined it. How do users assess quality—and, by implication, good design? Table 6.2 presents six distinct levels of satisfaction in the user's experience.[6]

Each level on the software quality ladder involves a skill level of computational thinking. The lowest levels are undisciplined use of CT; the highest levels are disciplined CT to design for customer practices, breakdowns, and evolving concerns. The higher the level, the more professional and advanced aspects of CT are involved. Ascending the ladder, CT skill extends its sensibilities from formal requirements to customer concerns and futures; the level of customer satisfaction rises.

Level –1: No Trust

Customers do not trust the software. It may be buggy, crash their systems, hold their data for ransom, or carry malware. One might think customers would avoid untrusted software. But instead they do often use untrusted

Table 6.2 Levels of Software Quality and Satisfaction Assessments

	Quality Level	Skill level of CT
4	Software delights	Design software to anticipate evolution of customer practices and concerns after using the software
3	Software produces no negative consequences	Design software to avoid potential customer breakdowns
2	Software fits environment	Design software to align seamlessly with customer practices and social norms
1	Software fulfills all basic promises	Design software to meet all customer requirements via disciplined use of programming and software engineering CT
0	Some trust, begrudging use, cynical satisfaction	Design software with indifference toward the customer, modest CT discipline
−1	No trusts	Exploit the customer, little CT discipline

software—often after being lured by fraudulent pitches, phishing, visits to compromised websites, overwhelming desires for convenience, and the like. Programs at this level are often cobbled together without serious thought to the DRUSS objectives and many are aimed at exploiting customer weaknesses.

Level 0: Cynical Satisfaction
Many customers trust some but not all the claims made by the software maker—enough to be cynically willing to

use it. Much software is released with bugs and security vulnerabilities, which the developers fix only after hearing customer complaints and bug reports. User forums are rife with stories about how the software has failed them and with requests for workarounds and fixes; representatives of the developers are usually nowhere to be seen in these forums.

Using some intermediate CT practices, developers get their software working despite design flaws and holes that demand workarounds. The developers may tolerate their disorganized and haphazard development environment because they are under strong pressure to get something workable to market before the competition, they believe that customers will tolerate many bugs, and they evade liability with no-responsibility license agreements customers must sign to unlock software. This approach is common in the software industry. It is coming under fire because the many bugs are also security vulnerabilities. Cynical customers have no loyalty and will desert to another producer who makes a better offer.

Level 1: Software Fulfills All Basic Promises
The customer assesses that the producer has delivered exactly what was promised and agreed to. This level of basic integrity relies on more advanced programming and software engineering CT. The ISO standard addresses this level well. Software developers at this level are often

standards-oriented and their practices are aimed at producing consistent, reliable products.

Level 2: Software Fits Environment

At this level, the design extends beyond meeting the stated requirements. It aims to align the software with existing customer practices and it honors cultural sensibilities and other social norms. The customer assesses that the software is a seamless fit to the customer's environment. The bank ATM is a good example of this kind of alignment. The ATM implements familiar bank transactions, enabling customers to use an ATM immediately without having to learn anything special or new. The customer has the experience that the software improves the customer's ability to get work done and to carry out important tasks.

Level 3: Software Produces No Negative Consequences

At this level, the designer has examined a range of possible ways that the software could produce breakdowns for the customers and builds in operating rules and checks to avoid them. After a period of use, customers encounter no unforeseen problems causing disruption or losses. Customers assess that the product's design has been well thought out and that it anticipates problems that were not apparent at the outset. The software does not produce negative consequences that often arise on the lower quality levels, such as vulnerabilities to hackers and malware, vulnerabilities to user mistakes without the provision to cancel actions or back out to a previous good state, interference with the organization's practices, wasted effort for only marginal productivity gains, and frustration with other negative consequences to customers or their organizations.

At this level, designers may also include functions that the customer did not ask for but that will spare future frustration. Continuous backup systems are one example; the user can retrieve any previous version of a file and can transfer an entire file system to a new computer quickly. Utilities that rebuild damaged files or directories are another example. Still another example are internal management controls that allow the designer to continue to work with the customer after the software is installed in order to modify the software in case negative consequences are discovered. These actions—anticipation of breakdowns and availability of repair services after delivery—are essential for a software producer to earn the user's satisfaction at this level. Programming and software engineering CT do not orient software developers to this direction; design-oriented CT is required.

Level 4: Software Delights

At the highest level the software goes well beyond the customer's expectations and produces new, unexpected, sometimes surprising positive effects. The user expresses great delight with the product and often promotes it among others. The customer assesses that the producer understands the customer's world and contributes to the customer's well-being. Programming and software engineering CT cannot approach this because delight cannot be stated as formal requirements.

Very few software systems have produced genuine delight. Some early examples include the UNIX system, which was elegant and enabled powerful operations with simple commands; the Apple Macintosh, which brought a revolutionary, easy-to-use desktop with a bitmapped display; the DEC VAX VMS, which was amazingly stable and retained previous versions of files for fast recovery; VisiCalc, the first automated spreadsheet, which made easy accounting available to anyone; Lotus 1-2-3, a successor of VisiCalc, which enabled arbitrary formulas in cells and opened a new programming paradigm; Microsoft Word, which made professional document formatting easy and eventually banished most other word processors from the market; and some smartphones, which provide a reasonably secure environment to download apps that customize the device to the user's taste and identity.

Some smartphone apps have attained high delight ratings; for example, many airlines, publishers, and newspapers offer apps that give direct access to their content via a mobile device. Some apps give users access to networks where data from many others are aggregated to give the user something that saves a lot of time and anxiety. For example, Amazon created the Kindle reader service that enables users to purchase ebooks from the Amazon store and begin reading them instantly from any device with a Kindle app. Google and Apple maps use location information from smartphones to detect traffic congestion, overlay it on street maps, and propose alternate routes around congested areas. Blizzard Entertainment accumulated as many as 10 million subscribers to its World of Warcraft online game because of its rich complexity, easy entry, and detailed graphics. Uber allows users to hail rides whose drivers come to their exact location within minutes. In each case customers found they could do previously impossible things with the app than without, well beyond their expectations.

The interesting thing about these examples is that many of them failed important ISO metrics such as portability, speed, efficiency, or reliability. Yet customers ignored those shortcomings and became avid and loyal subscribers to the software developer.

Software developers are banking on new delights as artificial intelligence technology matures. Many people are looking forward to driverless cars, personal assistants that know your daily routines and overcome your forgetfulness, and virtual reality tools that allow you to tour distant places, train risk-free for a new skill or environment, or access new kinds of entertainment. Computational thinking that takes design deep into the organizational, human, and social aspects of computing have never been as important as today.

But delight is ephemeral if based only on the software itself. Having mastered the new environment, customers will expand horizons and expect more. Few would find the original UNIX, Macintosh, VMS, VisiCalc, or Word to be delightful today. Software producers now invest considerable effort into knowing their customers and anticipating what will delight next.

The Design Way of Computational Thinking

The software engineering way of computational thinking emphasizes the correct implementation of clearly stated functional requirements in software. Its success measures are properties observable in the software or its usage data.

The design way of computational thinking also emphasizes the construction of virtual worlds in which users can inhabit and achieve some purpose that is meaningful to them. Its success measures are assessments of satisfaction and quality by users.

Software engineering CT is especially useful for large systems that must perform reliably in safety critical environments. People want carefully engineered air traffic control systems, nuclear plant control systems, and Mars rovers. Design CT is especially useful for software that must fit customer communities, facilitate adoption, and deliver great value. Design CT does not abandon software engineering CT; it listens for opportunities to include delightful functions customers have not yet asked for.

As we described earlier in this chapter, to characterize design CT we have proposed six levels at which customers assess software quality and satisfaction. Program correctness is essential but produces satisfaction only at the first level. The highest level, delight, arises in the context of the relationship between the customer and software developer. The delighted customer will say that the developer has taken the trouble to understand the customer's work and business, is available to help with problems and to seize opportunities, may share some risks on new ventures, and generally cares for the customer. Software developers today look to designs and services that produce genuine delight. When they succeed we witness new waves of killer apps.

COMPUTATIONAL SCIENCE

The sciences do not try to explain, they hardly even try
to interpret, they mainly make models.

—John von Neumann (1955)

Computational science refers to the branches of every
scientific field that specializes in using computation, such
as computational physics, bioinformatics, and digital humanities. Although numerical methods have been a feature
of science for centuries, simulation of complex systems
was rarely viable before computers. Scientists developed
mathematical models, usually expressed as sets of differential equations, but unless they could find closed-form
solutions to the equations, the complexity of the models
usually blocked them from any effective method to calculate the results. Although computers slowly began to invade all fields of science in the 1950s, the supercomputers

in the 1980s were a tipping point in mustering the computing power to solve a rapidly increasing number of these equations by simulation. This led to an explosion of simulation models in science, some of which made discoveries that earned Nobel Prizes. By the mid-1980s, many scientists were counting computer simulation as a new way to do science, alongside the traditional ways of theory and experiment.

In the 1980s, scientists from many fields came together to formulate "grand challenge problems"— problems for which their models gave solutions that required massive computations. By extrapolating Moore's law on the doubling chip speed every two years, they were able to predict with considerable accuracy when computation was going to yield solutions of these challenges. For example, aeronautics engineers projected that by 1995 they could design a safe commercial airliner using simulation as a substitute for wind tunnel testing—and the Boeing company achieved this with its 777 aircraft, which flew its first test flights in 1994.

Computer simulations got so good they could be used as experimental platforms. With simulations, scientists were able to explore the behavior of complex systems for which there were no analytical models. Simulations also opened the door for a new way of exploring the inner workings of the nature: by interpreting natural processes as information processes and simulating them in order to understand how they work.

The computational turn of science and its new methods and tools were widely adopted and the change was radical. Computational methods were described as the most significant scientific paradigm shift since quantum mechanics. The computational-science revolution ushered in a new wave of computational thinking. But unlike the previous waves of CT—which were initiated by computer scientists—scientists in other fields initiated the new CT wave. Computational science became a major driving force in the development of CT outside computing.

During the 1980s and the 1990s, computational thinking provided the mental toolbox for the new computational sciences—co-developed across many fields. In fields where natural phenomena could be interpreted as information processes, CT became a must-have skill for researchers. In an ironic twist, where previous scientists had argued that computing is not a science because there are no natural information processes, the new generation of computational scientists found information processes all over nature. And like computer scientists of the 1950s and 1960s, computational scientists learned CT from the practice of designing computations to explore phenomena and solve problems in their fields.

In this chapter, we describe how computational thinking became central to sciences, explain a number of CT practices in computational science, and discuss the new ways in which computational scientists interpret their subject matter. The electronic computing age brought some remarkable advances to science in three aspects: simulation, information interpretation of nature, and numerical methods.

Science and Computation: Old Friends

Science and computation have been old friends for centuries. Through most of the history of science and technology, two sorts of scientist roles have been common. One is the experimenter, who gathers data to explore and isolate phenomena, describe recurrences, and reveal when a hypothesis works and when it does not. The other is the theoretician, who designs mathematical models to explain what is already known and uses the models to make predictions about what is not known. The two roles were active in the sciences well before computers came on the scene.

Both roles used computation. The experimenters produced data that had to be analyzed, classified, and fit to known mathematically formulated laws. The theoreticians used calculus to formulate mathematical models of physical processes. In either case, they could not deal with very large problems because the computations were too extensive and complex.

A third role emerged: scientists who saw new opportunities using computers as simulators that neither the experimenters nor the theoreticians used. The computing pioneers at the Moore School, home of the ENIAC, argued early on that computer simulation could make any computer into a laboratory. They saw the evaluation of models and the production of data for analysis as a new frontier of science. Crossing that frontier required new ways of incorporating modeling and simulation into research, as well as new kinds of computational thinking directly relevant to science.

Large-scale modeling and simulation required significant upgrades to mathematical software. Numerical analysts, a branch of early computer scientists, were heavily involved in the quest to improve mathematical software to efficiently calculate mathematical models on computers. They were especially concerned with representing numbers and performing long calculations in machines that could only offer finite precision; controlling round-off errors and increasing computational speed were major concerns.

In the late 1980s, John Rice, a pioneer of mathematical software, estimated that mathematical software had improved in performance by a factor of 10^{12} since the 1950s. Of that improvement, 10^6 was due to faster hardware and another 10^6 due to better algorithms. Moore's law was only part of the reason numerical methods got better. The ingenuity of the numerical analysts did the rest.

The idea of using calculus to evaluate mathematical models must have seemed obvious to the modelers because their equations were typically differential equations. Many physical processes could be described by relating the value of a function at a point to the values of the function at neighboring points. For example, a modeler who knew that the rate of change of function $f(t)$ was another function $g(t)$ could calculate the values of $f(t)$ in a series of small time steps of size Δt with the difference equation $f(t+\Delta t) = f(t) + g(t)\Delta t$. The sequence of Δt-separated time points is a time-series sample of the function. This idea is easily extended to functions over space coordinates (x,y) by relating $f(x,y)$ to $f(x+\Delta x,y)$ and $f(x,y+\Delta y)$ on a two-dimensional grid. John von Neumann, the polymath who helped design the first stored program computers, described algorithms for solving systems of differential equations on discrete grids.

Because of the complexity of computations involved in these simulations, high-performance supercomputers became very important in the sciences. Only those computers had sufficient power to numerically solve differential equations over complex grids. With supercomputers, computational scientists cracked the grand challenge problems articulated in the late 1980s.

For centuries, theory and experiment were the two modes of doing science. Supercomputers changed this, opening a new approach to doing science based on computational exploration and modeling. It was the most significant scientific paradigm shift since quantum mechanics. The computational science revolution ushered in a new wave of computational thinking.

As computing invaded science, something unexpected happened. Instead of computing becoming more like other sciences, other sciences became more like computing. Scientists who used computers found themselves thinking differently—computationally—and routinely designing new ways to advance science. By simulating air flows around a wing with the Navier-Stokes equation discretized to a grid surrounding an aircraft, aeronautical engineers eliminated the need for wind tunnels and many test flights. Astronomers simulated the collisions of galaxies. Macroeconomists simulated scenarios in national and global economies. Chemists simulated the deterioration of space probe heat shields on entering an atmosphere. Simulation allowed scientists to reach where theory and experiment could not. It became a new way of doing science. Scientists became computational explorers as well as experimenters and theoreticians.

Just as numerical analysis enabled better simulation, better simulation enabled another new scientific paradigm: information process interpretation of phenomena

For centuries, theory and experiment were the two modes of doing science. Supercomputers changed this, opening a new approach to doing science based on computational exploration and modeling. It was the most significant scientific paradigm shift since quantum mechanics. The computational science revolution ushered in a new wave of computational thinking.

in the world. Much can be learned about a physical process by interpreting it as an information process and simulating the information process on a computer. For example, it has become a mainstay of modern biology, notably with sequencing and editing genes.[1] For the quantities modeled, the real process behaves as if it were an information process. The simulation and interpretive approaches are often combined, as when the information process provides a simulation for the physical process it models.

The term "computational science" and its associated term "computational thinking" came into use during the 1980s. In 1982, Kenneth Wilson received a Nobel Prize in physics for developing computational models that produced startling new discoveries about phase changes in materials. He designed computational methods to evaluate the equations of renormalization groups, which he used to observe how a material changes phase, such as the direction of the magnetic force in a ferrimagnet. He launched a campaign to win recognition and respect for computational science. He argued that all scientific disciplines had "grand challenge" problems that would yield to massive computation.[2] He and other visionaries used the term "computational science" for the emerging branches of science that made computation their primary method. Many of them saw computation as a new paradigm of science, complementing the traditional paradigms of theory and experiment. Convinced by the benefits computational thinking would bring to science, they launched a political movement to secure funding for computational science research, culminating in the High Performance Computing Act (HPCA) passed in 1991 by the US Congress, and bringing computational thinking in science into public view.

It is noteworthy that computational science and computational thinking in science emerged from within the scientific fields—they were not imported from computer science. In fact, computer scientists were slow to join the movement. Whereas numerical analysts often felt like outcasts from mathematics in the 1950s, and outcasts from computing in the 1970s, they were natural participants in computational science. Fortunately, this mood did not last; numerical analysts are important members of the computing field.

Computation has proved so productive for advancement of science and for engineering that virtually every field of science and engineering has developed a "computational" branch. In many fields the computational branch has grown to be critical for the field. For example, biology is seen as an information science.[3] Chemists design molecules and simulate them to find out how they would fare under real conditions. Pharmaceutical companies test molecules by simulation to learn if they would be effective against certain diseases. Computational methods are spreading into traditionally non-experimental fields, such as humanities and social sciences. This trend will continue. Computation will invade deeper into every field.

Because CT has advanced science—by providing better methods of numerical analysis, advanced simulations, and the information interpretation of physical processes—many people will decide to learn the skills required of computational designers and thinkers.

Computational Thinking in Science

Computational thinking in science has two aspects. First, mental skills facilitate the design of computational models for natural processes and for methods of evaluating models. The phrase "modeling and simulation" comes up frequently for this aspect of CT in science. Computing terminology gained favor among computational scientists because it distinguished the new computational methods of conducting science from the traditional methods of theory and experiment.

The second aspect of CT in science is a skill of interpreting the world in terms of information processes. Instead of asking computing's question—Can an information process be efficiently automated?—computational scientists ask: Can a simulated information process replicate a real process? What kind of information process creates an observed phenomenon? What computational mechanism is behind an observed process? For instance, many biologists study DNA and protein interactions in terms of information processes with the hope of designing future DNA that heals diseases and lengthens life. Physicists hope that by interpreting physics as information processes, they can learn about hard-to-detect particles from simulations of particles.

We see then that CT in computational science has a different orientation from CT in computer science. Much of computational science is concerned with using modeling and simulation to explore phenomena, test hypotheses, and make predictions in its respective fields. Much of computer science is concerned with designing algorithms to solve problems. Scientists and engineers who design simulations are often not formulating problem statements; they are investigating the behaviors of phenomena. Computing people are often not using simulations to understand how nature works; they are designing software to do jobs for users.

Computing people and scientists looking to collaborate ought to keep this distinction in mind. The collaboration will work better if the computer people develop an understanding of the science domain, and the scientists an understanding of the computing domain. For example, one of us (Peter) personally witnessed a disconnect between computational and computer scientists in the 1980s. A team of PhD computational fluid dynamics scientists invited PhD computer scientists to join them, only to discover that the computer scientists did not understand enough fluid dynamics to be useful. They were not able to think computational fluid dynamics with the same facility as the fluid dynamicists. The fluid dynamics scientists wound up treating the computer scientists like programmers rather than peers, much to the chagrin of the computer scientists.

Computational Models

The term "computational model" can also be a source of misunderstanding. To a scientist, computational models are sets of equations, often differential equations, that describe a physical process; the equations can be used computationally to generate numerical data about the process. Simulations are often the algorithms that do this. In contrast, a computational model in computing means an abstract machine that runs programs written in a programming language. The Turing machine is frequently cited in computing as the fundamental theoretical model of all computation, even though it is too primitive to be useful for most purposes.

Scientists routinely use abstract machines in the computing sense because every one of the familiar programming languages is associated with an abstract machine. For example, the FORTRAN language presents an abstract machine that is particularly good at evaluating mathematical expressions. The Java language presents an abstract machine that hosts a large number of autonomous "objects" that concurrently send and receive messages from each other. The C++ language also has objects but is closer to the actual machine and thus gives more efficient executable code.

The computational models in computational science are realized as abstract machines that bring a replica of a natural information process to life. The simulations are the executions of programs that implement those abstract machines.

Modeling and Simulation

Computational science has a rich trove of methods for modeling, simulating, and interpreting natural processes. We will consider five examples that illustrate the range and we will point out some key CT features of the models and the simulations.

Mandelbrot Set

Many simulations walk through all the points on a grid, computing a function at each point, and then visualizing the result by assigning colors to the numbers on the grid points. The Mandelbrot set is a good example of a computation that reveals behaviors no one suspected by inspecting the equations. In the Mandelbrot visualization, for each point on a grid, the computer calculates a series of values based on a simple equation over complex numbers, and assigns colors to those points: if the calculated series converges (stays within some limits), color the point black, and if the series diverges, color it blue or yellow. Now repeat this for all points on the grid.[4]

When each point's color is assigned to a pixel, the Mandelbrot set appears on a graphics screen. No one suspected that such a simple computation would yield such a beautiful, mysterious object (see the figure below). One

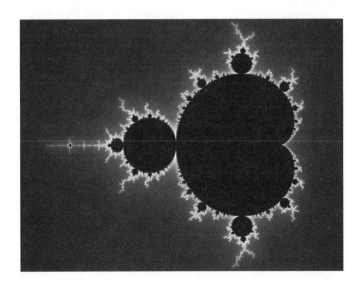

can select a small square anywhere on the graphic, zoom in on it, cover it with a grid and calculate all its grid-point colors—and see more copies of the Mandelbrot set appear at smaller scales. Each new zoom reveals more sets. It never ends. Mandelbrot called this self-replicating behavior at all scales "fractals."

The fractal idea (self-similarity at different scales of measurement) was the key to Ken Wilson's renormalization group algorithms that yielded new discoveries in physics when simulated on a supercomputer, and it won him a Nobel Prize. The fractal idea is used in visualization systems to compute realistic graphic images, such as trees or horizons, rapidly.

Telephone Engineers

When the first telephone exchanges were designed in the early 1900s, telephone engineers confronted a serious design issue. In a town of K customers, there are potentially K^2 connections. Guaranteeing every customer could connect to any other customer at any time they desired would be hopelessly complex and expensive, especially since most of the time most of the customers are not talking at all. To control the complexity and cost, engineers decided to build switches that would handle up to N calls at once (N is substantially less than K). This of course brings a risk that a customer cannot get a dial tone if the exchange is already carrying N calls. The design question was how to choose

N so that the probability of encountering the busy signal is small, for example 0.001. A random walk computational model yields an answer. The model has states n = 0, 1, 2, ... , N representing the number of calls in progress up to a maximum of N, here N = 10. Requests to initiate new calls are occurring randomly at rate λ. Individual callers hang up randomly at rate μ. Each new-call arrival increases the state by 1 and each hang-up decreases it by 1. The state diagram in the figure below represents the movement through the possible states. Telephone engineers define $p(n)$ the fraction of time the system is in state n and can prove a difference equation $p(n) = (\lambda/n\mu)p(n-1)$. They calculate all the probabilities by guessing $p(0)$, calculating each $p(n)$ from its predecessor $p(n-1)$, and then normalizing so that the sum of all $p(n)$ is 1. Then they find the largest N so that $p(N)$ is below the target threshold. For example, if they find $p(N)$ = 0.001 when N = 10, they predict that a new caller has a chance 0.001 of not getting a dial tone when the exchange capacity is 10 calls.

A key idea here was modeling the physical process with a state space representing all the possible states of the system, connected by transitions representing the random rates of flow between pairs of states. By invoking

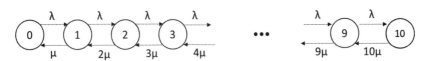

a flow balance principle—total flow into a state equals total flow out—engineers got a set of equations relating the proportions of time $p(s)$ each state s is occupied. They can then calculate the values of $p(s)$ by applying the equations. This form of modeling is very common in queueing theory and system performance evaluation because all the measures of interest, such as throughput, response time, and overflow probabilities, are easy to calculate from the $p(s)$.

Doctor's Waiting Room

Engineers have also used state space models to build controllers of systems. In this example (see the figure below), a doctor wishes to build an electronic controller for her office, which consists of a four-person waiting room and a one-person treatment room. Patients enter the waiting room and sit down. As soon as the doctor is free, she calls the next patient into the treatment room. When done, the patient departs by a separate door. The doctor wants an

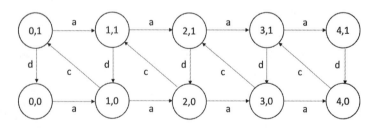

indicator lamp to glow in the treatment room when patients are waiting, and another to glow in the waiting room when she is busy treating someone. The engineer designing the controller uses a computational model with states (n,t) where $n = 0,1,2,3,4$ is the number in the waiting room and $t = 0,1$ is the number in the treatment room. The controller implements the state diagram above. The indicator lamp in the treatment room glows whenever $n > 0$, and the lamp in the waiting room whenever $t > 0$. State transitions occur at three events: patient arrival (a), patient departure (d), and patient called by the doctor (c). Sensors located in the three office doors signal these events.

In this case the model is not used to evaluate probabilities of state occupancies, but to plan the states and transitions of an electronic circuit. It is of course possible to interpret the state diagram as in the previous example, where a, b, and c are flow rates between the states.

Aircraft Simulation
Aeronautics engineers use simulations from computational fluid dynamics to model airflows around proposed aircraft. They have become so good at this that they can test new aircraft designs without wind tunnels and space shuttle designs without test flights. The first step is to build a 3-D mesh of the space surrounding the aircraft (see the figure on the following page). The spacing of the grid points is smaller near the fuselage where the changes

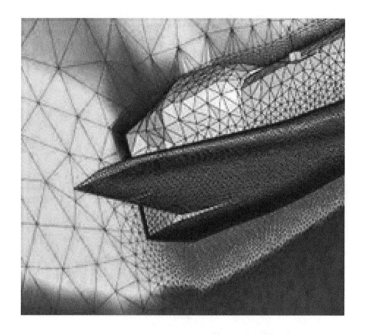

in air movement are greatest. Then the differential equations of airflow are converted to difference equations on the mesh, and a supercomputer grinds out the profiles of the flow field and forces on each part of the aircraft over time. The numerical results are converted to shaded images (as shown in the figure on the next page) to visualize where the stresses on the aircraft are greatest.

This form of modeling is common in science. A physical process is modeled as differential equations that relate

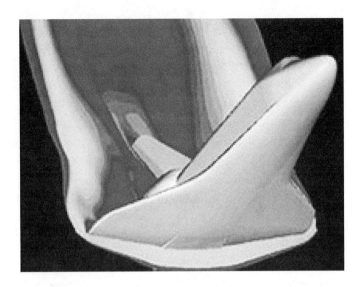

the values of the process at a point in space to the values of the process at close neighbors. The space in which the process is to be studied is modeled with a mesh. The difference equation is used to relate each mesh point value to its immediate neighbors. A graphical display converts the field of values on the grid to a colored picture. The whole mesh can be recomputed for the next time step, giving an animated visualization.

Genetic Algorithms
Since the 1950s, various geneticists experimented with computer simulations of biological evolution, studying

how various traits are passed on and how a population evolves to adapt to its circumstances. In 1975 John Holland adapted the idea of these simulations as a general method for finding near optimal solutions to complex problems in many domains. The idea, depicted in the flow diagram in the figure below, is to develop a population of candidate solutions to the problem, encoded as bit-strings. Each bit-string is evaluated by a fitness function and the most-fit members of the population are selected for reproduction by mutation and crossover. A bit-string is modified by mutation when one or several of its bits are randomly flipped. A pair of bit-strings are modified by

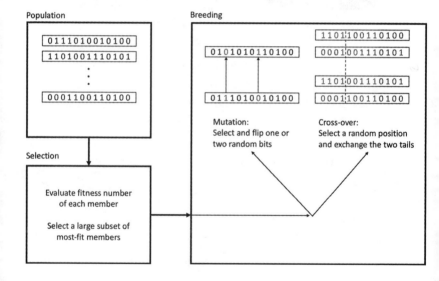

crossover by selecting a random breakpoint and exchanging the two tails of the strings. This generates a new population. The process is iterated many times until there are no further improvements in the most-fit individuals or until the computational budget is exhausted. This process is surprisingly good at finding near-optimal solutions to optimization problems whose direct solutions would otherwise be intractable.

Grand Challenges and Wicked Problems

Computing has changed dramatically since the time when computational modeling grew up. In the 1980s, the hosting system for grand-challenge models was a supercomputer. Today the hosting system is *the cloud*—a massively distributed system of data and processing resources around the world. Commercial cloud services allow users to mobilize immense storage and processing power they need just when they need it. In addition, users are no longer constrained to deal with finite computations—those that start, compute, deliver their output, and stop. Instead devices now tap endless flows of data and processing power as needed and users count on the whole thing to keep operating indefinitely. With so much cheap, massive computing power, more people can be computational designers and tackle grand-challenge problems.

Yet there are important limits to what all this computing power can do. One limit is that most computational methods have a sharp focus—they are very good at the particular task for which they were designed, but not for seemingly similar tasks. That limit can often be overcome with a new design that closes a gap in the old design. Facial recognition is an example. A decade ago, methods of detecting and recognizing faces in images were not very good—people had to look at the images themselves. Today, deep learning (neural network) algorithms have been used to design very reliable automated face recognizers, overcoming the earlier gap. These recognizers are trained by showing them a large number of cases of labeled images. But recognizers are "fragile" in the sense that no one knows how the machine will do when presented with inputs outside the training sets. Overcoming fragility has motivated computational scientists to look at machines that learn without training sets. A recent example is a machine that learned to play the board game Go by competing against other machines, eventually becoming good enough to beat the world's highest-ranked Go player in a five-game match.

Self-learning machines have raised another concern: explainability. Designers and users want to know how the machine reached its conclusion. The idea that a machine can reach a conclusion makes sense when algorithms are seen as step-by-step procedures because the result can be explained by examining the steps followed. But when the algorithms are not step-by-step procedures, as with face recognizers and Go, that is not possible. All there is inside is an inscrutable, complex mass of connections. It is really the same problem with fellow humans—how do we explain why we do certain things? If asked directly, we may not know, and it certainly cannot be figured out by dissecting our brains. Other ways are needed to know when machines can be trusted and when not. Machine learning–related computational thinking is still in its infancy.

Another limit to what can be done with computing power concerns the many problems that cannot be solved at all with computation. We gave examples in chapter 3, which are either not computational at all, or so complex that they are forever beyond any computing power we can muster. But complexity is not the only barrier. Another is that some problems are inherently outside of science and technology and cannot be solved by scientific and technological methods. A favorite category is "wicked problems"—especially issues in the interactions of social communities and technologies. They defy solution when factions have enough power to defeat a proposal they dislike but not enough power to form a consensus. Examples are many: Millions of "clean" cars collectively produce unhealthy smog in dense cities. New information technology fosters the growth of income inequality where designers reap much more bounty than users. STEM education struggles to learn how to prepare students to face great uncertainty about the future of work, societal safety nets, technology, and climate change. The solutions to these problems are not scientific, technical, or computational but will emerge from social cooperation among the groups that now offer competing and conflicting approaches. Although computational thinking can help by visualizing the large-scale effects of individual actions, only social consensus and social action can resolve wicked problems.

Computational thinking is a powerful force within science. It emphasizes the "computational way" of doing science and makes its practitioners into skilled computational designers (and thinkers) in their fields of science. It brings forth new information interpretations in a diversity of disciplines. Computational thinkers in sciences spend much of their time modeling physical processes, designing solution methods for those processes, running simulations, and visualizing the results.

TEACHING COMPUTATIONAL THINKING FOR ALL

My basic idea is that programming is the most powerful medium of developing the sophisticated and rigorous thinking needed for mathematics, for grammar, for physics, for statistics, and all the "hard" subjects. Maybe I would even include philosophy and historical analysis. In short, I believe more than ever that programming should be a key part of the intellectual development of people growing up.

—Seymour Papert (Papert, 2005)

Through the 1990s, CT education was mostly the purview of universities; very little CT education was available elsewhere. Pre-college K–12 schools had a scattering of computer courses; most focused on computer literacy and a handful on programming. A tipping point came after 2000 when many people saw how pervasive computing was in everyday work and home life. Educators and policymakers began to agree that understanding the mechanisms of digitalization is an important 21st-century skill.

The previously obscure notion of the algorithm entered everyday conversation as people cited value they had received from algorithms on their web searches, income tax preparation, online shopping, spreadsheets, neatly formatted documents, display-ready presentations, and computerized courses, and then later on smartphones, social networks, ride hailing, short-term renting, dating, finding friends, and much more. It seemed that understanding how it all works is central for coping in the modern world. It was finally time to bring computing to the K–12 level of education.

Computing Education

Getting computing education to K–12 schools was a struggle of a whole different order from getting computing education into universities. Numerous pilot projects to introduce computers in schools foundered because few teachers had any experience with computers and there was little political support in school boards. By the 1980s, a sea change began as more parents and teachers acquired home computers and came to see the growing importance of computing in their own work. The "computer literacy"

Getting computing education to K-12 schools was a struggle of a whole different order from getting computing education into universities. Courses on computer literacy, later fluency, did not take hold. A computational thinking movement started in 2006 that energized educators and school boards to bring computer courses into all K-12 schools.

courses introduced at that time were generally disappointing from the CT perspective because they focused on the use of tools like word processors and spreadsheets, not on programming.

In the late 1990s, at the same time when the internet started to become a household commodity, a new education movement favoring "fluency with information technology" over literacy gained momentum and was supported by a popular textbook of the same name. It was an attractive notion that fluency with language and practices of computing would be a powerful asset in the emerging digitalized world. Bringing computing education to schools would enable children to become smart users of computing technology and would introduce them to the limitations and risks of algorithmic processes behind emerging functions such as online purchasing, Internet searching, news services, communication, and later social media. Despite its attraction, the fluency movement did not produce a widespread change in computing education in K–12 schools.

Then, in 2006, Jeannette Wing proposed that computational thinking is what everyone wants; not literacy or fluency.[1] She struck a resonant chord. In the next several years at the US National Science Foundation (NSF), she mobilized $48 million in resources and convinced many people to bring computer courses into all K–12 schools. Their major successes included getting education organizations to issue definitions of CT and associated curricula at different grade levels; training teachers in CS principles; starting a new family of CS-principles introductory courses at universities; and developing a new Advanced Placement curriculum and exam to interface high schools to these new introductory courses. CT went mainstream.

But as suggested above, this success was not easy. School boards in K–12 institutions had a long history of reluctance to add a computing curriculum in their schools. The CT movement brought a turn of mind to many school boards. Without that movement, we would not be talking about computational thinking in K–12 education at the scale we do it today. In this chapter, we will interpret the progression of computing education as a series of waves that started with the form of CT available in the 1950s (algorithmizing and mathematical problem solving), moved to Papert's *Mindstorms*, then to literacy and fluency, and culminated most recently in a modern version of CT designed for children in schools.

General-Purpose Thinking Tools?

Academic education for automatic computing machinery began in the late 1940s, when computing pioneers started educational programs on numerical methods for computing on large-scale machines. These early efforts went mainstream in the 1950s when the mass production of stored-program computers created a demand for a large number of people who could program them. After the early entry by private companies, university educators started organizing conferences to discuss computing education in the mid-1950s. By 1960, some 150 US universities offered some training in computing. There was, however, no standard view on what people needed to know about computing; individual programs depended on local idiosyncrasies such as specific jobs, needs of businesses, personal agendas of the faculty, research contracts, and other stakeholder interests.[2]

Already in those early days some computing educators described their visions of computing as a *thinking tool for learning*—a tool to deal with problems and questions in many fields besides computer science. Alan Perlis, who founded the computer science department at Carnegie Mellon University, was an outspoken advocate for this vision. He said that computing would be automating processes in many fields, and people in those fields would be "algorithmizing." With this term, he referred to mental skills for reasoning about problems and developing computational solutions. George Forsythe cited Perlis in his 1958 address for the Mathematical Association of America: "Whereas we *think* we know something when we learn it, and are *convinced* we know it when we can teach it, the fact is that we don't *really* know it until we can code it for an automatic computer!" A decade later, Forsythe echoed the claim that computing provides general-purpose mental tools that would serve a person for a lifetime. Both Perlis and Forsythe firmly believed that everyone in every field will benefit from learning computing's procedural ways of doing things. They believed that computational models would be useful in all fields.

The visions of computing education grew ever more ambitious about what CT will be able to achieve. Marvin Minsky, a famous pioneer in artificial intelligence, argued, in his 1969 Turing Award speech, that computing would surpass mathematics in importance for early education.[3] Donald Knuth, a pioneer in understanding algorithms, argued that teaching a computer to do something forces precision and leads to deeper understanding than traditional means of thinking.[4] Another pioneer argued that the modern successor to "the classical person" would be "Turing's person."[5] Two famous computing educators wrote that computing's procedural epistemology is creating a revolution in how people think and express themselves.[6] All this optimism about computing skills transferring to general problem solving turned out to be premature, as we discuss next.

CT Is Not Easily Transferable

The first wave of bringing CT to K–12 schools focused on programming. In the mid-1960s, some US high schools got DEC PDP-8 minicomputers and enterprising teachers organized courses around them. Numerous initiatives for using computers in schools over the 1960s and 1970s led to a few notable innovations. For example, the Little Man Computer for teaching machine languages and computers to students was introduced in 1965; one of the early programming languages for children, Logo, was introduced in 1967; and the famous concept for *Dynabook*, a children's portable computer, was born in 1968. Although minicomputers and some microcomputers were common in the late 1970s, educators, lacking financial resources and political will, were unable to transform the pilot courses into a large-scale rollout to schools.

The Logo programming language was a standout among the many initiatives of the 1960s. It was not a stand-alone, general programming language. It was a part of an integrated framework of pedagogical, technological, and educational ideas designed by Seymour Papert based in his deeply grounded understanding of how children learn. His 1980 book *Mindstorms*, written after a decade of research and experimentation with Logo, was a milestone for computing education and teaching computational thinking. Papert coined the phrase "computational thinking" for the practice of procedural thinking he taught to children. He argued that learning is most effective when learners "construct knowledge"—they acquire practices from being immersed in a world of practices. They build their knowledge from practicing it rather than being told. The learning theory of constructionism became very popular in education. Papert continued to advocate self-directed learning, project learning, meaningful representations, facilitation-based education, and the use of technology to support learning in the classroom. His ideas influenced the Lego company to design and market the children's programmable bricks called Lego Mindstorms.

Teaching fundamental computational thinking skills, such as programming and computer modeling, is much harder than teaching spreadsheets, word processing, and other application tools of computing. Despite the popularity of constructionism, the central idea of *Mindstorms*— the shift from "learning to program" to "programming to learn"—was hard to market among teachers. How could we achieve universal teaching of computational thinking without enough willing teachers? Could we rely on a smaller set of interested teachers to teach everybody?

The hope that a small number of teachers could teach CT to everybody was paired with the *transfer hypothesis*. The hypothesis is a belief that CT is a metacognitive skill learned from programming; students who learn CT in one domain became better problem-solvers in other domains, too. This belief bolstered the position that teaching computing should be an essential element of K–12 education. The most enthusiastic supporters of the hypothesis made claims such as "the concept of procedure is the secret educators have so long been seeking," and "the pedagogic value of algorithmic approach aids in the understanding of concepts of all kinds." They argued that teaching programming improves generic thinking skills such as logical thinking and generally "sharpens the mind." The transfer hypothesis would indeed be important if it could be validated.

Critics of the transfer hypothesis referred to a research base in developmental cognitive science, arguing that there was no evidence of skill-transfer from programming to other subjects. Research with adults did not support transfer of cognitive skills between domains. Programming itself is a complex network of skills including mathematical abilities, conditional reasoning, analogical reasoning, procedural thinking, temporal reasoning, and memory capacity. It was not clear which parts of this complex transferred or not. After much detailed investigation, education researchers eventually concluded there is not enough evidence to accept the transfer hypothesis. It was not compelling as a justification to teach computing in K–12 schools.

Given that the transfer hypothesis does not work, schools needed more teachers who understood CT and could teach it in different contexts. Few teachers understood computers well enough to do this. Teaching a computer literacy course might be within their reach, but that baby step would not qualify them to teach CT. In the mid-2000s, when the US NSF began supporting the training of more computing teachers, the shortage of qualified teachers began to abate.

From Literacy to Fluency

The early advocates of algorithmic thinking would be appalled at many of the "computer literacy" courses in the 1980s and 1990s, which focused on how to use desktop applications, such as word processors, spreadsheets, and sketchpads. Motivated students and teachers found these courses boring. Literacy with desktop software was a far cry from their aspirations to participate in and shape the computer revolution. The professional societies, including ACM, IEEE-CS, and the British Computer Society, offered to help K–12 educators develop computer courses with more depth, but got little buy-in. In 1999, a US National Research Council commission upped the ante, reframing the question from literacy to fluency. Fluency offered capabilities, concepts, and skills essential for some levels of computational thinking. The NRC initiative was paired with a textbook *Fluency with Information Technology* that became quite popular among high school teachers.

Many schools brought computing into their curricula for pragmatic reasons as they responded to demands from parents and school boards. They sought access to simulations and other teaching software, access to basic programming, participation in the Internet revolution, learning 21st-century skills, preparation for employment in STEM fields, broadened social participation, and a new means for children to express individual creativity.[7] Educators and parents were disposed toward these goals because they believed that learning programming teaches important skills no other subject does, and because they did not want their children to be at a disadvantage in a world increasingly dependent on skills with information and communication technology.

In the 2000s, the entry of programming and computational design into schools was also easier because of advances in programming methodology and technology and changes in what entry-level programmers needed to know. New languages such as Python were much easier to use and hid well the underlying details of the operating system and hardware. Graphical, drag-and-drop user interfaces were very successful. Powerful tools automated significant parts of the programming process.

With all these advancements in programming languages, tools, and methods, programming was accessible to more students and teachers than ever before. There were more opportunities for becoming fluent in computing. But even so, in 2010 many schools had no computer courses or Advanced Placement curriculum in computing. Gaining fluency was not powerful enough to be a driving force.

Computational Thinking Revived

Jeannette Wing's 2006 essay on computational thinking launched a new wave in the movement to provide computing courses for all students in K–12 schools. The term *computational thinking* resonated and inspired action where literacy and fluency had not. Wing mobilized significant resources at the NSF to bring a large number of researchers into investigations of CT in education, to train a large number of teachers for teaching CT, to mobilize private organizations to produce K–12 curriculum recommendations for CT, and to develop a new Advanced Placement curriculum and exam on computing principles. Wing's essay became one of the most cited in computing education, a rallying point in a global movement to penetrate CT into K–12 education.

Major organizations including CSTA (Computer Science Teachers Association), the British CAS (Computing at School), Code.org, and the Australian ACARA2 (Australian Curriculum, Assessment, and Reporting Authority) developed and recommended curriculum frameworks for K–12 CT. These organizations promoted coding clubs, coding boot camps, and the international movement called "Hour of Code." CT became a key word gathering hundreds of thousands of hits in news stories, blog postings, book chapters, articles, research projects, and essays on computing education.

The rapid infusion of so many enthusiastic newcomers who were unfamiliar with the long prior history of CT led to considerable confusion about definitions and learning objectives of CT. Some invented new CT frameworks for K–12 schools from scratch, imperfectly reinventing ideas that had been discussed for decades, omitting important ideas, confusing CT with the use of applications, and incorporating into their dogma some serious misconceptions about computing and algorithms. This resulted in a variety of tensions between different groups that used CT.[8] Here are the some of the most common points of contention, many of which can be explained by differences between CT for beginners and CT for professionals—basic CT in K–12 is surely different from advanced CT in higher education—as well as different contexts of application:

1. Whether CT is limited to thinking about the mechanics of constructing algorithms—or includes thinking about machines, computational science, software engineering, and design.

2. Whether CT is mostly about programming—or also encompasses systems, networks, and architectures; or whether it is not really about any of those.

3. Whether the definition, that CT is the formulation of algorithms to solve problems, is too narrow a view of CT's scope.

4. Whether algorithms are only those that fit the strict definition from the theory of computing—or whether algorithms could also be more loosely defined.

5. Whether algorithms necessarily include an abstract machine in the background.

6. Whether algorithms are primarily directions for controlling machines—or are primarily means of expressing procedures.

7. Whether using computational tools teaches CT.

8. Whether carrying out daily step-by-step procedures is a manifestation of CT.

9. Whether CT is learned from practicing programming— or from well-designed learning activities that use steps and rules.

10. Whether learning CT in the context of computing transfers to problem-solving skills in other fields.

11. Whether CT is domain dependent—or is a meta-skill valid in all domains.

12. Whether computational processes are found in nature—or whether they are limited to algorithms and machines.

13. Whether information processing by computers differs from information processing done by humans—and whether "information processing agents" can include things such as molecules, DNA, or quarks.

14. Whether students' learning should be assessed from their demonstrating skill at designing computations—or from their knowledge of certain key concepts.

15. Whether satisfaction of customers with the job that software does should be part of the assessment of software success.

16. Whether K–12 CT education has to stick with strict definitions of computing—or could for pragmatic and pedagogical reasons take some liberties.

We have expressed our stance on these questions at various points throughout this book. We see CT as an old, rich human practice that has been perfected in the modern age of the electronic computer. We see CT as a mental discipline for thinking about designing computations of all kinds, a skill at the advanced levels honed and improved through extensive practice and experience. We see many different levels and styles of CT from basic computing skills and insights to highly advanced, specialized ones. We see that there are many good ways for teaching entry level CT. We see that ultimately nearly all CT will boil down to machine-realizability. We see CT as mostly domain dependent—for example, how you think about computation in biology is different from physics, chemistry, or humanities. We see as wishful the notion that CT is an innate human ability exercised daily by using computational tools and performing routine everyday procedures. We see the attempt to define algorithms as a set of possibly ambiguous steps resolved by human computers as a misunderstanding of computing.

We would like to point out one other movement to bring computing into K–12 schools. Known as CS Unplugged,[9] it seeks to teach computing concepts and practices through games, magic tricks, and activities. It was founded in the late 1990s by Tim Bell, Michael Fellows, and Ian Whitten. It has gained a worldwide following and influenced the design of the ACM K–12 and code.org curriculum recommendations.

In summary, we see plenty of room for a broad, pluralistic approach to teaching computational thinking while remaining faithful to computing's well-honed disciplinary ways of thinking and practicing. Most of all, we hope that all teachers of computing bring their students a good sense of the richness and beauty of the many dimensions of computation.

FUTURE COMPUTATION

Technology is part of our civilization. Sometimes people talk about conflict between humans and machines, and you can see that in a lot of science fiction. But the machines we're creating are not some invasion from Mars. We create these tools to expand our own reach.
—Ray Kurzweil (2013)

Computational thinking is an ongoing quest to capture computing's ways of thinking and practicing. It is in never-ending flux, constantly renewing itself. Although many of the central CT precepts are very old, evolution of computing practice and technological state-of-the-art have affected how we see CT and what is central to CT. For instance, ever-evolving software development suites, new languages, and cloud services are shifting computational design tasks away from lower-level programming operations toward higher and higher levels of abstraction—thereby making computing jobs more design-intensive. Traditional programming is losing its role as the primary interface to computations; instead, domain-specific and intelligent tools are enabling more and more users to harness the potential of computers without programming them. CT expands well beyond programming and software development.

We will discuss some of the forces that are shaping our world and their likely effects on how we see computing and think about it. We will also discuss some important questions that CT cannot help us with. CT has its limits.

New Computational Models

One of the most obvious reasons why CT is changing is that computing technologies are changing. Throughout the long reign of Moore's law for silicon chips, the basic architecture of chips in computers and mobile devices has remained true to the von Neumann design from 1945—separate memory and processing units, with a processor stepping through instructions stored in memory. The notion of "computational steps" in the modern definitions of CT comes from this design as well as from Alan Turing's definitions of computing.

But Moore's law cannot be sustained because of the physics of silicon and the nature of the chip-making process.[1] For this reason, researchers have been searching for new technologies that might supersede silicon-based von Neumann architectures and continue the exponential growth rate of information processing speed. Quantum computers, neural networks, reversible computers, DNA computers, memristor computers, and a few others are prime candidates. Each technology defines a new computational model that is the target for designers.

Consider, for instance, the D-wave, a commercial quantum computer.[2] It is designed to solve a set of equations, well known in physics as the Ising Model, which describe how certain systems settle into minimum energy states. *Programming* a D-wave computer means to encode the problem as a set of Ising equations and to input the coefficients into the machine; *execution* means to let the machine settle into a minimum energy state corresponding to the solution of the equations (a few microseconds); *readout* consists of reading the qubits (quantum bits) of the machine and interpreting them as the answer. There is no concept here of an "instruction set" or of programming as "designing a sequence of steps." Most computer scientists, on being shown how to set up the D-wave machine for the first time, experience a mind tilt—the process is nothing like the programming process they have known all their professional lives.[3] Trained physicists have much less trouble understanding the machine. The current working definition of CT—formulating a problem so that it can be solved as a series of computational steps—fails to describe the computational thinking this machine involves.

DNA computing is another technology being investigated. In 1994 researchers performed an experiment in which they encoded possible paths in a map into strands of DNA, and then used the chemical methods of the day to evolve the initial mixture into one where the majority of strands represented the shortest tour of the map.[4] Considerable progress has been made with this technology. In 2016, another research team used the modern CRISPR gene editing technique to insert an image into the DNA of a bacterium. Computer scientists trained to think in terms of computational steps have more trouble than molecular biologists understanding how DNA computing works.

These examples illustrate CT has expanded beyond the idea of problem solving with computational steps. Our broader definition—designing computations that get computers to do jobs for us, as well as explaining and interpreting the world as a complex of information processes—is closer to the mark.

Design

The ongoing increase in the importance of design is another reason CT is changing. Computational thinking is no longer confined to developing programs and algorithms to solve computational problems. Only a small portion of apps development, for example, is concerned with algorithms; the bulk of the work focuses on design of systems to deal with the concerns of a community. Design in this sense is an ongoing interaction between designers and users, watching their reactions to prototype software, evaluating what works and what does not work, and adapting the software accordingly. This is a much broader view of design than the "blueprint," the "plan," or the "setup of an experiment" views of early programming and software engineering communities. It is a skill set that combines sensibilities to moods and histories in communities with deep knowledge of existing technologies and other useful components. Design requires understanding humans in their communities as much as it requires understanding technology.

One effect of new designs in computing has been the automation of many cognitive tasks that as recently as a decade ago were considered out of reach of computing machinery. This kind of automation is displacing workers and has caused great concern that many current jobs could be automated, putting many people out of work. The flip side of the coin, however, is that the new technologies breed new problems that require new designs—creating new jobs for designers.

Computational design is now a skill that you can have in any field besides your primary disciplinary skills. You do not have to be a computer scientist to be a computational designer. Computational design captures the spirit of today's computing revolution better than computational thinking does. Past technology revolutions showed us that the new technologies ultimately created more jobs than they displaced. The current computing revolutions in machine learning and app development are producing new jobs for designers while rendering obsolete some existing jobs by automating them. To help smooth the transitions, governments should help more with training and education programs so that displaced workers can learn the design skills of the new jobs.

The new emphasis on design is rejuvenating the engineering aspect of computing, which is much more sensitive to design than the science side is. The engineering side brings to computational thinking concerns about reliability, fault tolerance, architecture, and systems that are sidelined in the theory- and algorithm-oriented definitions of CT. What is more, it brings to CT human concerns, such as recognizing the social worlds that are embracing computing, adopting a design into a community's practice, recognizing ethical issues brought forth by technology side effects, and providing means that human judgment and care influence the actions of machines.

Machine Learning

Neural networks, first articulated in the 1940s as possible models for electronic computers, have become the main technology behind artificial intelligence (AI) and data analytics today. The neural network was a mathematical model in which a neuron "fired" when the combination of signals from other neurons exceeded its built-in threshold; the "fired" neuron entered an excited state that was then communicated to other neurons. The motivation for imitating the brain was that automatic computers might do human tasks better when built of similar components. Of course, a circuit of these neuron models is nothing like a real brain. The logic circuits of the first computers ran much faster than neural circuits. Today the situation is different: we now know how to use cheap graphics cards to speed up neural network calculations. IBM and Intel now market chips that are even faster; they recognize that a new way of thinking is needed to put their chips to best use and they offer courses in the operation and use of their chips.

Early neural networks were small and easily confused when presented with new inputs not in their training sets. Modern neural networks consist of many layers, have much higher capacity, and are less easily confused. Thanks to graphics processing chips, trained neural networks of many layers respond to inputs almost instantaneously. Since layers, nodes, and connection weights do not change after the network is trained, performance does not depend on the data input. As neural network implementations typically do not have loops, they run in a constant time with constant memory spaces. That means that neural networks can be used in real-time applications with deadlines much more reliably than traditional programs.

A big attraction of neural networks is that they are "trained" rather than "programmed." For example, we do not have very reliable algorithms for face recognition, but neural networks can be trained to recognize given faces quite reliably. These networks are often called "self-programmed" because no programmer specifies the internal weights—although the weight-adjusting algorithm used in training can be viewed as an automatic programmer. For many problems, it is much easier to find or create suitable training data than to write a rule-based program. As mentioned in previous chapters, a big issue with neural networks is that there is no way to "explain" how the network generated an output, as is possible with traditional programs. Knowing the reasons behind a conclusion is important in many application areas such as medical diagnosis; neural networks confound that. CT has already had to adjust to include the tools used to build and train neural networks. Bigger challenges lie ahead with assessing the reliability and security of neural networks.

Another big attraction is that neural networks can be trained by having them interact with other neural networks instead of given data sets. The network for AlphaGo, which beat the world champion Go player in 2017, was trained by having it play against another AlphaGo network; it learned Go from play rather than from training on a large set of recorded Go games. This way of training networks by letting them learn from each other has the potential to be game changing.

Human-Computer Teaming

Garry Kasparov, the world champion chess grandmaster, was defeated in 1997 by IBM's Deep Blue computer. That game marks a milestone in chess because it was the first time a computer program beat a grandmaster. Kasparov had played several previous matches against lesser computers, winning them all.

Kasparov did not declare the game of chess dead. Instead, he invented a new kind of chess, Advanced Chess. In Advanced Chess, the two players of a match are each assisted by a computer. Before committing to the next move, the human player consults the computer program to gain insights into the possible effects of moves. The computer-assisted chess players played better chess than when they played without computers, but also better chess than computers alone played.

The notion that a human-computer team can always perform better than a very good machine is controversial. There are reports of recent Advanced Chess tournaments in which teams did poorly compared to matches between computers without humans. In medicine, diagnosticians teamed with computers do not always perform as well as the very best diagnostic computer.

Still, human-computer teaming has attracted a lot of attention in artificial intelligence research because it is capable of performing computations that no human or computer could do alone. An early example of this was the labeling of digital images with searchable keywords. Doing it by hand was far too slow to be useful for labeling images online. In 2006, Luis von Ahn of Carnegie Mellon University invented an online game where thousands of pairs of humans labeled the images presented to them; if their keywords matched, their labeled image went into the searchable database. The "labeling function" implemented by these human-computer teams had been thought to be non-computable. The human computer teams were more powerful than computers.

Human-computer teaming requires a different kind of computational thinking than traditional computer programming. We watch with great interest how the controversy over whether teams can outperform machines plays out in the future.

Technology Jumping

In 2006 Ray Kurzweil, a futurist and inventor of computing technologies, prophesied that by 2030 we will be able to build a computer the size of the brain, with the same number of neurons and connections as the brain.[5] Such a computer would, he envisioned, develop its own consciousness and superintelligence. How such computers would treat humanity is an unanswerable question. The best that can be said is that the new machines would have such different concerns from ours that we cannot fathom how they would treat us. That moment of their creation is called the singularity because of the utter unpredictability of what lies after an artificial intelligence develops consciousness.

Kurzweil arrived at his conclusion by extrapolating Moore's law, the prediction of Gordon Moore in 1965 that silicon chips would double in capacity about every two years for the same price. The computer chip industry has followed the law by doubling power every two years for over half a century. In many ways Moore's law is a triumph of computational thinking because chip engineers needed to think hard to find ever better ways to build computing circuits.

Kurzweil exploited the phenomenon of technology jumping in his analysis. Since the beginning of the information age in the early 1900s, he argued, the same doubling effect was observed in the technologies of the day, for example punched card machines or vacuum tube machines. When one technology could no longer produce the two-year doubling, another took over. Moore's law for silicon is actually the fifth wave of technologies displaying two-year doubling. Kurzweil has confidently predicted that more technology jumps will occur and sustain the trend, allowing him to predict the processing power available by 2030 and beyond, and arrive at the singularity.

Technology jumping is a standard practice of the computing industry. The adoption of a particular technology versus time almost always follows an S-curve with exponential growth until an inflection point, after which the growth slows down as the market saturates. Business leaders are sensitive to inflection points because a competitor with a better, exponentially growing technology can upend their businesses when their own growth slows. They try to anticipate inflection points by developing new technology in their research labs and jumping to it when their business reaches the inflection point. They can then ride the new technology wave during its exponential growth stage.

Although the singularity is a product of computing and computational thinking, it cannot be addressed with computational thinking, and we cannot improve our understanding of it through computational thinking.

The Whole World Is a Computer Hypothesis

Some scientists have argued that information is the basis of all physics. Every particle and every interaction is the product of information flows and exchanges at a more fundamental level than the smallest particles known. In 2002, Stephen Wolfram, a physicist and inventor of the Mathematica program—a triumph of computational thinking in itself—published a big book in support of this claim.[6] In 2003, Nick Bostrom, a philosopher, argued for a possibility that we are characters in a simulation run by a much more intelligent species studying their ancestors. While other physicists see some merit in the claim that all particles and interactions can be explained with quantum mechanical probability waves, which are forms of information, they regard the idea that our world is a digital simulation as far-fetched.[7]

The whole-world-is-computer hypothesis appeals to those who believe that computational thinking and computing are pervasive without limits.

Ideological Fights over What Should Be Taught

There is a never-ending debate on what should be taught in a computing curriculum. There are two hot spots in the debate. One concerns the selection of programming language and programming framework that students should be introduced to. Should it be a language that is easy to learn and has the least-confusing structure and syntax, such as Python? Or should it be a language that is used by their future employers in industry, such as Java or Javascript? What are the benefits of starting with a framework that treats programs as sources of instructions for a machine (known as an "imperative" framework) compared to one treating programs as compositions of functions (known as a "functional" framework)? These debates have been a staple of computing faculty meetings since the 1960s and are not likely to abate in the years ahead.

The other hot spot is the tension between the ideals of science-mathematics and of engineering-design. The science-mathematics ideal teaches abstractions of things in the world and leaves it to the student to apply the abstraction to the case at hand. The engineering-design ideal focuses on all the details that a builder has to get right for the resulting program to be safe and reliable. The science-math view has had the upper hand for many years, but with the rise of design, the engineering view is gaining new currency. In reality, both traditions are important for the success of computing: the science and engineering sides need each other.

Reflection on the Emerging World

We write this book at the 50th anniversary of the first recommendations for developing a computing curriculum made by the ACM (Association for Computing Machinery), a society of computing professionals that we both belong to. That curriculum and its subsequent specifications were shaped by many factors noted in the previous chapters:

• Strong emphasis on technology development from the beginning.

• Wide resistance to forming computing departments from other academic departments that did not accept computing as a legitimate field.

• Developing a computing community network at the dawn of the internet era.

- Being torn by intense debates over the roles of science, math, and engineering in computing, manifested as struggles over how to teach software engineering and information technology, and how much to trust formal methods for software development.

- Coming to grips with the emergence of computational science and now the penetration of computing into nearly every field of human endeavor.

- The deaths and resurrections of artificial intelligence and its claims about automation and the future of humanity.

This battle-hardened inheritance does not help us with many of the pressing issues of the world emerging around us. The worldwide connectivity we helped bring about through the Internet has brought many benefits from shrinking the world and globalizing trade. But it has also spawned conflicts between non-state organizations and traditional nations, trade wars, protectionism, terrorism, widespread detachment, fake news, misinformation and disinformation, political polarization, and considerable unease and uncertainty about how to move in the world. Access to troves of information via the Internet has begun to show us that knowledge does not confer wisdom, and we long for wise leaders who have yet to appear. The promise of respectful information society enabled by the

Internet has turned into polarized society enabled by social media. The world we encounter in our daily lives is full of surprises, unexpected events, and contingencies that not even our best learning machines and data analytics can help us with. We are now finding that many resources including sea and air access are contested among nations; we lack means to resolve the resulting disputes and we worry that the resulting conflicts could trigger wars or economic collapses. We see that collective human action affects the global environment but have yet to find ways to protect our environment we will bequeath to our children and grandchildren.

This leaves us with a big question: how shall we shape computing education so that our graduates can develop the design sensibilities, wisdom, and caring they will need to navigate in this world, of which they will be citizens? Our current curriculum, chock full of courses covering the 2013 body of knowledge, is not up to this task.

A place to start would be to open up space in our crowded curriculum to have conversations on big questions about the consequences of computing throughout the world. These conversations need to be interdisciplinary and intergenerational. Their purpose would not be to solve problems but think together—to edify—to develop mutual understanding, appreciation, and respect around these issues. Some examples of big questions ripe for edifying conversations attending computational thinking are:

Our battle-hardened notions of computational thinking do not help with many of the pressing issues of the world emerging around us. Access to troves of information via the Internet has begun to show us that knowledge does not confer wisdom.

- What cannot be automated? What should be automated? How far can automation take us? Who gets to decide what is automated and what is not?

- How can AI generate more jobs through automation than it displaces?

- How can we help people whose jobs are displaced by software and hardware we have designed?

- How do we cultivate good designers?

- How can we increase trust on decisions by neural networks when given inputs outside their training sets?

- How will we discourage the development of an automated surveillance society?

- What technological solutions can be found to the cybersecurity problem?

- How do we make our world work when computers have been embedded into almost all devices connected to the global network?

- How does digital technology affect global politics, nationalism, balance of trade, climate change, and other issues of globalization?

- In what ways will blockchains and cryptocurrencies affect our problems with trust in central authorities? Are they too expensive to maintain?

- How do we protect societies that are deeply dependent on computing from an attack on a critical component of infrastructure, like the electric grid or the Internet?

- How do we prepare people to appreciate the difference between wisdom and abundance of information?

- What are the social implications of brain-computer interfaces and neural implants into our brains and bodies?

- What economic avalanches are possible because multiple, interdependent technologies are dropping in cost exponentially?

We do not believe any of us has answers to any of these questions. But we need to be having the conversations about them. In so doing we need to embrace the mathematicians, scientists, sociologists, philosophers, anthropologists, lawyers, engineers, and everyone else in our field. It is time for us to think together about the design and impacts of our technology and so shape our future with wisdom and understanding. It is time to give up the old tensions that we inherited from times long past, and work together as brothers and sisters, mothers and fathers, old and young on these big questions.

EPILOGUE: LESSONS LEARNED

In the research for this book, we learned a few lessons that are worth summarizing here.

Lesson 1: CT is an addition, not a replacement.
Everyone thinks their own field's ways of thinking (and practicing) are valuable and worthy of learning in many other fields. Enthusiasts want to spread the gospel of success to other disciplines. The list of "thinkings" to be spread is long: computational thinking, logical thinking, economic thinking, systems thinking, physics thinking, mathematical thinking, engineering thinking, design thinking, computational thinking, and more.

Our conclusion is that computational thinking is often a welcome addition to other fields, but not a replacement for their ways of thinking and not a meta-skill for all fields.

Lesson 2: CT is an old, well studied, and diverse topic.
The term "computational thinking" (CT) became popular after the US National Science Foundation included it in a funding call in 2007. For many people it was the first time they heard arguments about the value of computing in education. CT seemed to be a new invention, a

breakthrough portending a revolution in K–12 education. The truth is, human beings have been doing CT for over 4500 years. It has been advocated for K–12 education since the 1960s.

Some of the first "CT for K–12" curriculum designers attempted to build a "body of knowledge" for CT from scratch without being informed by the long history of computational thinking, including similar attempts to bring computing to schools. They unwittingly created some conceptual errors in their claims about the capabilities and character of CT. We are concerned because inflated expectations and conceptual problems can easily become a part of the CT folklore, and it may take years to dispel them. We urge computing educators to turn to the massive existing body of computing education research to clean this up.

Lesson 3: The speed of computers is the main enabler of the computing revolution.

Most of what software does for us is made possible by the incomprehensible speed gap between computers and humans—billions to trillions times faster. Even though humans can execute computational steps, they could not carry out most of these computations in their lifetimes. The machines can literally do the humanly impossible. While it is true that humans can personally perform algorithms for some information processing tasks, the revolutions of the computer age are not about where people can perform algorithms in their own lives, but about what computers are able to do for them.

Lesson 4: Advanced CT is domain dependent.
For advanced tasks, you need to understand the domain in which you want to figure out how to get a computer to do a job for you. For example, an expert programmer who knows nothing about quantum physics will have little to offer to a team of physicists working on a quantum computer. Similarly, working with the nature's complex algorithms in biology requires considerable understanding of biological processes. Algorithmic models in chemistry require deep familiarity with the corresponding chemical processes. Building an information system for a hospital requires extensive understanding of the institutional, informational, and workflow processes in the hospital context. Much of advanced computational thinking is context-specific and tightly tied to the application domain.

Lesson 5: CT has changed the tools, methods, and epistemology of science.
Computational thinking has fostered a revolution in science. Scientists in all fields have found that CT is a new method of doing science, different from the classic methods of theory and experiment. They came to this discovery

in the 1980s when they began using supercomputers to crack scientific "grand challenges." This was a profound paradigm shift that enabled many new scientific discoveries. Each field developed its own strain of CT that was not imported from computer science. Computer science CT has been enriched by its collaboration with the computational sciences.

Lesson 6: The public face of CT is that of elementary CT.
CT is billed for K–12 curriculum purposes as a set of concepts and rules for programming. But many professionals see CT as a design skill, and many natural scientists see it as an advanced method of scientific interpretation. Like all skills, you can be a beginner, advanced beginner, competent, proficient, expert, or master. Many debates about what CT "really" is seem to collapse different skill levels of CT within the same debate. For example, K–12 teachers argue for curricula that are almost solely aimed at beginners and that contain a small, teachable set of CT insights, practices, and skills. Other advocates argue for CT as advanced, professional skills that require many years of practice and experience. Failing to make the distinction leads to conflicts—for example, the hype about how learning programming opens career paths is silent about what professional computational designers do. Education efforts are important on all levels from K–12 through university and beyond.

Lesson 7: Beginner and professional CT together comprise a rich tapestry of computational thought.

Educators in K–12 schools have developed an impressive "CT for beginners"—insights and methods for teaching computing to newcomers. Professional software systems designers and scientists have developed an impressive "CT for professionals"—advanced methods for designing and building complex software that works reliably and safely, and for conducting scientific investigations. The synergy between these two aspects of computational thinking has propelled the computer revolution.

Lesson 8: Change is an inseparable part of CT.

There has never been a consensus about what computational thinking "really" is. There may never be a full consensus. During every decade in the modern history of computing there would be different answers to questions about the essence of computational thinking. Advances in computing keep computational thinking in constant change. We should embrace the lack of a fixed definition as a sign of the vitality of the field rather than our own failure to understand an eternal truth.

GLOSSARY

Abstraction
Simplifying complex phenomena by representing only their salient features, while omitting or hiding details.

Algorithm
Description of a method to compute a function, or more broadly, to solve a category of computational problems. All the steps are so precisely specified that a machine can perform them.

Artificial intelligence (AI)
The subfield of computer science that investigates whether computers powered by appropriate software can be intelligent (strong AI), or whether computers can simulate human cognitive tasks with information processes (weak AI).

Automation
Using machines to replace human controllers of physical processes (such as chemical plants or manufacturing lines), to perform knowledge-work processes (such as reviewing documents or processing invoices), or to build a computer to perform a task, replacing humans who formerly performed the task.

Bit and Byte
A bit is the smallest unit of information that distinguishes between something being present (1) or not present (0). A byte is a set of 8 bits, allowing 128 possible combinations of 8 bits. Large enough combinations of bits can stand for anything that can be represented by discrete values, such as numbers, characters, patterns on a display, or colors.

Boolean algebra
The set of expressions that can be formed from logic variables (each representing a single true-false bit) combined with operators such as OR, AND, and NOT. Boolean expressions are used in programming languages to specify conditions under which a statement will be executed. They are also used to describe the functions of logic circuits inside computers.

Central processing unit (CPU)

The hardware component of a computer that fetches and executes elementary instructions such as ADD, SUBTRACT, GO-TO, and COMPARE, and decides on what instructions are executed next. Other hardware components of a computer include the memory (which stores all data and instructions) and the input-output interface (which connects with the outside world).

Cloud, The

A worldwide network of storage systems and processing systems that can be accessed from anywhere just when and as needed. Users who rent data storage and processing time do not know where their data are physically stored and processed.

Compiler

A software program that translates programs written in a high-level programming language meant for humans into binary machine code meant for the processor.

Computational complexity

A subfield of computer science that investigates the intrinsic difficulty of solving problems. Difficulty is measured by the computational steps and memory space needed. Some problems like searching a list for a name are "easy" because they can be computed in time directly proportional to the length of the list. Some problems like finding the shortest tour of a set of cities are "hard" because in the worst case they require enumerating and measuring all the possible tours, the time for which grows exponentially fast as the number of cities and roads grows.

Computational model

The description of an abstract machine that performs algorithms—for example, a conventional computer chip that executes machine instructions one at a time, a neural network that recognizes faces in images, or a quantum computer that cracks cryptographic codes. In science and engineering, it also refers to a mathematical model of a physical process, which can be simulated or evaluated by a computer.

Computer

An entity, human or machine, that can perform calculations and symbol manipulations according to a set of precisely specified rules. From the 1600s to the 1930s, "computer" meant "a person who computes." The first electronic computers in the 1940s were called "automatic computers." The adjective "automatic" was dropped by the 1950s.

Data abstraction
A practice that originated with programmers in the 1960s to encapsulate a complicated data structure behind a simple interface. Users could access the data only through the interface; they could not directly access the memory holding the data. The view of the data seen through the interface is much simplified—hence the word abstraction. An example is a file, which looks to a user as a container of a linear string of bits; the interface allows only reading and writing. The actual file may be implemented as a set of blocks scattered around the storage medium, all hidden from the user.

Decision problem
A famous problem from mathematical logic in the early 1900s. Given a logical system consisting of axioms and rules for constructing proofs of propositions, is there an algorithm that will decide whether a given proposition is true? For a long time mathematicians believed there was such a procedure, but could not find it. In the 1930s a number of mathematicians, working independently from each other, formally defined the concept of algorithm and showed that there is no general solution to the decision problem.

Decomposition
Breaking a complex thing down to simpler, smaller parts that are easier to manage. In software, the parts become modules that are plugged together via interfaces.

Digitization
The work of constructing a binary coded representation of an entity. The representation could be processed by a computer. For example, the wave form of speech can be sampled 20,000 times a second, each sample producing a reading of the wave's amplitude and encoding it as a 16-bit value. The digitized speech can then be stored and processed on a computer.

DRUSS objectives
In software engineering, software systems that are dependable, reliable, usable, safe, and secure.

Encapsulation

Using interfaces to hide inner mechanisms and internal information from outside users in order to improve reusability, access restriction, protection of information from user errors, and maintainability.

Fractal

A term coined by mathematician Benoit Mandelbrot for sets that are self-similar at different scales. For example, the coast line of a country looks ragged in a satellite photo; it still looks ragged from a hang glider; and it still looks ragged under an up-close view of a wave rippling over the sand. Fractals have been used in graphics to draw complex objects from simple forms that can be repeated at all scales.

Generalization

Extending a solution to a broader class of similar problems.

Graphics processing unit (GPU)

A chip included in a computer to run the graphical display. Modern GPUs can hold 3D representations of objects and can rotate them to any angle or slide them to any distance computationally, then project the resulting image on to the 2D screen, all in real time.

Heuristics

Procedures for finding approximate solutions to computationally intractable problems. For example, in chess we evaluate proposed moves by a point-counting system for pieces lost; that is much less computing-intensive than enumerating all possible future chessboards. Good heuristics give solutions that are very good most of the time.

if-then-else construct

A form of statement in a programming language that selects between two or more alternative paths in program code. For example, "if sum≥0 then color sum-value black else color sum-value red" is used by accountants to highlight negative numbers in red on their spreadsheets.

Intuition

An aspect of embodied expertise where the expert is able to know immediately how to deal with a situation, based on extensive past experience. The expert may know what to do but cannot explain why.

Logarithm

In mathematics, the logarithm of a given number is the exponent to which a fixed base must be raised to produce that number. Thus, the log-base-2 of 8 is 3 because $2^3=8$. Logarithms are useful for multiplying numbers since the product of two numbers adds their exponents. Take, for example, multiplying 8 by 16. Because $2^3 \times 2^4 = 2^7$, we can take the base-2 logs of the two terms (here 3 and 4, respectively), add the logs (yielding 7), and raise the base 2 to the power of the resulting log (here 2^7). Slide rules multiply by adding the logs of the two multiplicands.

Logic circuits

The basic electronic circuits in a computer. They combine binary signals with operations AND, OR, and NOT and store the results in registers, which are processed by more logic circuits in the next clock cycle.

Machine code

The instructions of an algorithm encoded into binary codes that a computer can recognize and execute.

Neural network

A form of circuit that takes a very large bit pattern as input (such as the 12 megapixels in a photograph) and produces an output (such as faces recognized in the photo). The components of the network are designed to be loosely similar to the neurons in the brain. The network learns by being trained rather than being programmed.

Operating system

The control program that runs a computer system. It allows users to log in and access their data, protects user data from being accessed by others without permission, schedules the resources (CPU, disks, memory) among competing users, and provides an environment in which users can run their programs.

Qubits

The basic elements of a quantum computer. They are the quantum-world analog of bits in a conventional computer, but they have a peculiar property called superposition, which means they can be in the 0 and 1 states simultaneously. Superposition significantly increases their representational and computing power. They are represented by electron spins or magnetic fields.

Race conditions

Many electronic circuits have multiple paths connecting an input to a particular output. If a change of the input travels at different speeds over the different paths, the value of the output can fluctuate randomly depending on the order the signals arrive. That random fluctuation can cause malfunctions in downstream circuits that use the output. Race conditions can also appear in operating systems where two users attempt simultaneous access to a file and the final value of the file depends on which one went last.

Registers

Processor registers are the basic building blocks of storage within a CPU. A register consists of a set of flip-flops, which are small circuits that can store a 0 or 1. Thus, an 8-bit register is made of 8 flip-flops. The CPU instructions combine values in registers and store their results in other registers.

Representation

Computing relies heavily on one thing standing for (representing) something else. Computations require information to be represented in a digital form, such as two values of voltage in circuits or the presence or absence of perturbations on materials. We use 0 and 1 to represent those physical phenomena.

Simulation

Computer simulations rely on computational models of phenomena to track the behavior of those phenomena over time. The elements of a model are theories, variables, equations, parameters, and other known features of the phenomenon in order to faithfully characterize the modeled system. Simulation uses these model elements to see how the system changes from one time unit to the next.

Transfer hypothesis

The hypothesis that learning computational thinking in computer science transfers to problem-solving ability in other fields. The hypothesis would predict that a person who came to be a good problem solver in computer science would be able to solve problems in physics with the same expertise. There is little empirical evidence to support this hypothesis.

Truth values

The two allowed values "true" and "false" of a logic variable. When presented in numbers, "0" is typically interpreted as false and either "1" or any nonzero value as true.

Turing test

A test proposed in 1950 by Alan Turing to settle the question of whether a machine can think. A human observer carries on two text-based conversations, one via a connection to a computer, the other a connection to another human being. The observer does not know which is which. If the observer is unable to definitely identify the human (or machine) over a long period, the machine would be deemed intelligent.

Chapter 2

1. Davis (2012).

Chapter 4

1. Mahoney (2011);

2. Newell, Perlis, and Simon (1967).

3. Simon (1969).

4. Knuth (1974, 1985).

5. Dijkstra (1974).

6. Forsythe (1968).

7. Knuth (1985).

8. Guzdial (2014)

9. Arden (1980).

10. In his talk *A Logical Revolution,* Moshe Vardi describes the changing role and perceptions of logic in the field of computing, including the 1980s gloominess over what computers cannot do.

Chapter 5

1. Niklaus Wirth, software pioneer and the designer of the popular language Pascal, gives an excellent account of the development of programming practices and their supporting languages (Wirth 2008).

2. Stokes (1997).

3. Wilkes, in Metropolis, Howlett, and Rota (1980).

4. Wirth (2008).

5. Dijkstra (1980).

6. Saltzer and Schroeder (1975).

7. Alexander (1979).

8. Gamma et al. (1994).

9. Lampson (1983).

10. The levels principle was first used by Edsger Dijkstra in 1968 to organize the software of an operating system. It facilitated a correctness proof of the system because each level depended only on its components and the correctness of the lower levels, but not the higher levels. The discipline of designing a system as levels leads to much smaller and more easily verified systems.

Chapter 6

1. Forsythe (1966).
2. Grudin (1990).
3. Leveson (1995).
4. Parnas and Denning (2018).
5. Winograd (1983).
6. Denning (2016).

Chapter 7

1. Baltimore (2001).
2. Wilson (1989).
3. Baltimore (2001).
4. For the more mathematically inclined, the Mandelbrot set is the points in the complex plane at which the series of values of a function converges. A complex number is represented as $a+bi$, where $i=sqrt(-1)$ and $i^2 = -1$. The equation of the series is $z(n+1) = z^2(n)+c$ where $z(n)$ and c are complex numbers. Having chosen a value of c, compute a series of $z(n)$-values starting with $z(0)=c$. (You may need to go to an algebra refresher for algorithms to multiply complex numbers.) If the $z(n)$ sequence converges (stays within a short radius of c for all n), color the chosen value of c black. If it diverges color c blue or yellow. Now repeat this for all c points on a grid.

Chapter 8

1. Wing (2006)
2. Tedre, Simon, and Malmi (2018).
3. Minsky (1970)
4. Knuth (1974).
5. Bolter (1984)
6. Abelson and Sussman (1996)
7. Guzdial (2015)
8. Denning (2017).
9. See http://csfieldguide.org. nz and http://csunplugged.org.

Chapter 9

1. Denning and Lewis (2017).
2. McGeoch (2014).
3. See Walter Tichy's interview with Catherine McGeoch, *Ubiquity* July 2017, for a worked example of an Ising equation and its encoding into a form for the D-wave machine to solve, https://ubiquity.acm.org/article.cfm?id=3084688.

4. Adleman (1994).

5. Kurzweil (2006).

6. Wolfram (2002).

7. In April 2016, *Scientific American* magazine reported on a symposium of physicists and philosophers discussing the whole-world-is-computer hypothesis, giving the impression that they take more delight in entertaining themselves with the hypothesis than in the hypothesis itself. See https://www .scientificamerican.com/article/are-we-living-in-a-computer-simulation/.

REFERENCES AND FURTHER READING

Chapter 2
Davis, Martin. (2012). *The Universal Computer: The Road from Leibniz to Turing*. CRC Press.

Grier, David A. (2005). *When Computers Were Human*. Princeton University Press.

Hodges, Andrew. (1983). *Alan Turing: The Enigma*. Vintage Books.

Priestley, Mark. (2011). *A Science of Operations: Machines, Logic and the Invention of Programming*. Springer-Verlag.

Rapaport, William J. (2018). *Philosophy of Computer Science*. An online book draft, https://cse.buffalo.edu/~rapaport/Papers/phics.pdf.

Williams, Michael R. (1997). *A History of Computing Technology*. 2nd edition. IEEE Computer Society Press.

Chapter 3
Aspray, William, ed. (1990). *Computing Before Computers*. Iowa State University Press.

Campbell-Kelly, Martin, and William Aspray. (2004). *Computer: A History of the Information Machine*. 2nd edition. Westview Press.

Ceruzzi, Paul E. (2003). *A History of Modern Computing*. 2nd edition. MIT Press.

Cortada, J. W. (1993). *Before the Computer: IBM, NCR, Burroughs, and Remington Rand and the Industry They Created, 1865–1956*. Princeton University Press.

Williams, Michael R. (1997). *A History of Computing Technology*. 2nd edition. IEEE Computer Society Press.

Chapter 4
Arden, Bruce W., ed. (1980). *What Can Be Automated? Computer Science and Engineering Research Study*. MIT Press.

Daylight, Edgar G. (2012). *The Dawn of Software Engineering: From Turing to Dijkstra*. Lonely Scholar.

Dijkstra, Edsger. W. (1974). Programming as a discipline of mathematical nature. *American Mathematical Monthly* 81 (6): 608–612.

Knuth, Donald E. (1974). Computer science and its relation to mathematics. *American Mathematical Monthly* 81 (April): 323–343.

Knuth, Donald E. (1985). Algorithmic thinking and mathematical thinking. *American Mathematical Monthly* 92 (March): 170–181.

Mahoney, Michael Sean. (2011). *Histories of Computing*. Harvard University Press.

Metropolis, N., J. Howlett, and Gian-Carlo Rota, eds. (1980). *A History of Computing in the Twentieth Century: A Collection of Essays with Introductory Essay and Indexes*. Academic Press.

Newell, Alan, Alan J. Perlis, and Herbert A. Simon. (1967). Computer science. *Science* 157 (3795): 1373–1374.

Simon, Herbert A. (1969). *Sciences of the Artificial*. MIT Press.

Smith, Brian C. (1998). *On the Origin of Objects*. MIT Press.

Chapter 5

Alexander, Christopher. (1979). *The Timeless Way of Building*. Oxford University Press.

Brooks, Frederick P. Jr. (1975). *The Mythical Man-Month*. (20th anniversary edition, 1995). Addison-Wesley.

Brooks, Frederick P. Jr. (1987). No silver bullet: Essence and accidents of software engineering. *IEEE Computer* 20 (4): 10–19.

Campbell-Kelly, Martin. (2003). *From Airline Reservations to Sonic the Hedgehog*. MIT Press.

Denning, Peter. (2018). Interview with David Parnas. *Communications of ACM* 61 (6) (June).

Ensmenger, Nathan L. (2010). *The Computer Boys Take Over: Computers, Programmers, and the Politics of Technical Expertise*. MIT Press.

Gamma, Erich, Richard Helm, Ralph Johnson, and John Vlissides. (1994). *Design Patterns: Elements of Reusable Object-Oriented Software*. Addison-Wesley.

Koen, Billy V. (2003). *Discussion of the Method: Conducting the Engineer's Approach to Problem Solving*. Oxford University Press.

Lampson, Butler. (1983). Hints for computer system design. *Proc. ACM Symposium on Operating Systems Principles*, 33–48.

Metropolis, N., J. Howlett, and Gian-Carlo Rota, eds. (1980). *A History of Computing in the Twentieth Century: A Collection of Essays with Introductory Essay and Indexes*. Academic Press.

Mitcham, Carl. (1994). *Thinking Through Technology: The Path Between Engineering and Philosophy*. University of Chicago Press.

Saltzer, Jerome H., and Michael D. Schroeder. (1975). Protection of information computer systems. *Proceedings of the IEEE* 63 (9) (September): 1278–1308.

Stokes, Donald E. (1997). *Pasteur's Quadrant—Basic Science and Technological Innovation*. Brookings Institution Press.

Wirth, Niklaus. (2008). A brief history of software engineering. IEEE Annals of the History of Computing, 30 (3): 32–39.

Chapter 6

Brooks, Frederick P. Jr. (1975). *The Mythical Man-Month*. (20th anniversary edition, 1995). Addison-Wesley.

Denning, Peter. (2016). Software quality. *Communications of ACM* 59 (9) (September): 23–25.

Forsythe, George E. (1966). *A University's Educational Program in Computer Science*. Technical Report No. CS39, May 18, 1966. Stanford University: Computer Science Department, School of Humanities and Sciences.

Grudin, Jonathan. (1990). The computer reaches out: The historical continuity of interface design. In *CHI '90: Proceedings of the SIGCHI Conference on Human Factors in Computing Systems*, 261–268. ACM.

Landwehr, Carl, et al. 2017. Software Systems Engineering Programmes: A Capability Approach. *Journal of Systems and Software* 125: 354–364.

Leveson, Nancy. (1995). *SafeWare: System Safety and Computers*. Addison-Wesley.

Norman, Donald A. (1993). *Things That Make Us Smart*. Basic Books.

Norman, Donald A. (2013). *The Design of Everyday Things*. First edition 1983. Basic Books.

Parnas, Dave, and Peter Denning. (2018). An interview with Dave Parnas. *Communications of ACM* 61 (6).

Winograd, Terry, and Flores, F. (1987). *Understanding Computers and Cognition*. Addison-Wesley.

Chapter 7

Aho, Al. (2011). Computation and computational thinking.

Akera, Atshushi. (2007). *Calculating a Natural World: Scientists, Engineers, and Computers During the Rise of U.S. Cold War Research*. MIT Press.

Baltimore, David. (2001). How biology became an information science. In *The Invisible Future*. Peter Denning, ed., pp. 43–46. McGraw-Hill.

Denning, Peter. (2017). Remaining trouble spots with computational thinking. *Communications of the ACM* 60 (6) (June): 33–39.

Wilson, Ken. (1989). Grand challenges to computational science. In *Future Generation Computer Systems*, pp. 33–35. Elsevier.

Wolfram, Stephen. (2002). *A New Kind of Science*. Wolfram Media.

Chapter 8

Abelson, Harold, and Gerald J. Sussman. (1996). *Structure and Interpretation of Computer Programs*. 2nd edition. MIT Press.

Bolter, J. David. (1984). *Turing's Man: Western Culture in the Computer Age*. University of North Carolina Press.

Denning, Peter. (2017). Remaining trouble spots with computational thinking. *Communications of the ACM* 60 (6) (June): 33–39.

Guzdial, Mark. (2015). *Learner-Centered Design of Computing Education: Research on Computing for Everyone. Synthesis Lectures on Human-Centered Informatics*. Morgan & Claypool.

Kestenbaum, David. (2005). The challenges of IDC: What have we learned from our past? *Communications of the ACM* 48 (1): 35–38. [A conversation with Seymour Papert, Marvin Minsky, Alan Kay]

Knuth, Donald E. (1974). Computer science and its relation to mathematics. *American Mathematical Monthly* 81 (April): 323–343.

Lockwood, James, and Aidan Mooney. (2017). *Computational Thinking in Education: Where Does It Fit? A Systematic Literary Review.* Technical report, National University of Ireland Maynooth.

Minsky, Marvin. (1970). Form and content in computer science. *Journal of the ACM* 17 (2): 197–215.

Tedre, Matti, Simon, and Lauri Malmi. (2018). Changing aims of computing education: a historical survey. *Computer Science Education*, June.

Wing, Jeanette M. (2006). Computational thinking. *Communications of the ACM* 49 (3): 33–35.

Chapter 9

Adleman, Leonard M. (1994). Molecular computation of solutions to combinatorial problems. *Science* 266 (5187): 1021–1024.

Brynjolfsson, E., and McAfee, A. (2014). *The Second Machine Age: Work, Progress, and Prosperity in a Time of Brilliant Technologies.* W. W. Norton & Company.

Denning, Peter. J., and Ted G. Lewis. (2017). Exponential laws of computing growth. *Communications of ACM* 60 (1) (January): 54–65.

Friedman, Thomas. (2016). *Thank You for Being Late.* Farrar, Straus and Giroux.

Kelly, Kevin. (2017). *The Inevitable: Understanding the 12 Technological Forces That Will Shape Our Future.* Penguin Books.

Kurzweil, Ray. (2006). *The Singularity Is Near.* Penguin Books.

McGeoch, Catherine. (2014). *Adiabatic Quantum Computation and Quantum Annealing. Synthesis Series on Quantum Computing.* Morgan & Claypool.

Wolfram, Stephen. (2002). *A New Kind of Science.* Wolfram Media.

The MIT Press Essential Knowledge Series

PETER J. DENNING is Distinguished Professor of Computer Science, Chair of Computer Science Department, Naval Postgraduate School, Monterey, CA. MATTI TEDRE is Professor of Computer Science, University of Eastern Finland.